I0008767

The Art of Installation

and

The Science of Implementation

Project Management for
Package Software Implementation

Thomas F. Shubnell, Ph.D., FHIMSS

The Art of Installation and the Science of Implementation, Copyright ©2007, Thomas F. Shubnell, All rights reserved.

No part of this book may be used or reproduced in any form or by any means, or stored in a database or retrieval system without the prior written permission of the publisher, except in the case of brief quotations embodied in critical articles or reviews. Making copies of any part of this book for any purpose other than your own personal use is a violation of United States copyright laws. Entering any of the contents into a computer for mailing list or database purposes is strictly prohibited unless written authorization is obtained from the publisher.

Published by: LULU Press, Inc. 2007

Cover and interior design by Thomas F. Shubnell

ISBN: **978-1-4303-2433-1**

This book is dedicated to all my friends and acquaintances with whom I have had the pleasure to work beside and share some of our lessons learned.

TABLE OF CONTENTS

III

Introduction

The sad truth is that historically more projects have failed than have not failed. There have been many studies which detail specific reasons for project failure but most can be summed up to lack of planning and lack of leadership or management.

During the course of research for this book, I have discovered that project failures substantially occur because of failure to adhere to good business practices and common sense, not because of ignorance or stupidity. Large failures are brought about by fear and panic caused by small failures improperly reported or mitigated.

As information technology usage has evolved from wiring boards and manipulating machine language code for individual specific purpose uses to general purpose applications that are intended to be used by thousands of people. Project management as a discipline, has also evolved from single person projects to large complex projects involving hundreds of team members.

This new discipline requires new tools and new leaders. The new project leaders must be skilled and educated. They must possess inherent abilities to lead under duress as well as understand and communicate at any level in an organization. They must be born leaders and schooled tacticians with appropriate tools at their disposal and resources at the ready.

Real leaders are leaders by acclamation and managers by necessity. In order to properly lead, there must be a goal. In order to manage there must be something to manage. The tools are the plan and the methods by which a project will be conducted.

I have had installation and implementation projects done to me, by me, for me, and with me. Luckily, there have been many more successes than failures. It is likely due more to process than skill.

In life as in projects, we have rules to operate by. In life there are only ten rules. Some of us follow them and some do not. Projects have more than ten rules to be successful. Some of us follow them, some do not. In either case, the results are better if we follow the rules.

In life as in projects, some of us celebrate success along the way and some wait until it is too late to celebrate. Those that wait until it is too late never enjoy the fruits of their labor. The same is true for projects.

The time has come to elevate the project management process from the *art of installation to the science of implementation*.

Part A -
The Art

Chapter One - Background

The number of failed, late, and over budget software installations and implementations is staggering. Some statistics show the number of failed projects exceeds the number of successful installations by more than two to one. Reasons for these less than successful projects stem from each of the three major ingredients to any project; people, process, and technology.

In order for the profession to mature, project management responsibilities for the implementation process lifecycle of packaged software must evolve from the art of installation to the science of implementation.

> *The number of failed projects exceeds the number of successful installations by more than two to one.*

Installation includes the installation of package software without the accompanying process changes required to effect maximum utilization and benefit from the application system being installed.

Implementation includes the installation of packaged software as well as management of all of the people, processes, technology, and business changes required to exploit the software as designed.

Purpose

The purpose of this book is to synthesize data from current literature, web based information, surveys conducted, and industry best practices into a methodology capable of producing repeatable success for the implementation of package software.

Package software implementation processes were researched from inception through post-implementation review. Experiential data was gleaned from over thirty years of personal experience while implementing application software in the information technology industry.

Two surveys were developed and administered one year apart to persons who have been personally involved in the package software implementation process. Case studies and survey questionnaires were reviewed with users, vendors, and consultants who participated in package software implementation projects.

The scope begins with the processes immediately following pre-implementation planning. Although funding is extremely important to project success, this book does not include specific financial aspects of project management or ongoing budget issues as a part of the process.

The Problem

Project management for the implementation process of packaged software has not evolved to the point of consistent successful implementations.

Project managers are often unskilled for the job and untrained in requisites for success.

Project installation and implementation methodologies are myriad and many have been situationally developed. Therefore, they are incomplete for a full life cycle implementation. This has led to misuse of basic, sound practices, and processes required for successful implementation. In addition, project managers are often unskilled for the job and untrained in the requisites for success.

The Objective

The objective is to assemble the proven stages, phases, steps, etc., from many methodologies and to present a hybrid methodology based upon those existing methodologies as well as from professionals in the field, practical experience, and utilizing best practices.

This book contains descriptions of knowledge, skills, practices, and processes that can be applied for repeatable successful implementation of package software.

Project management and planning has been utilized in business for years to implement information systems but only recently has it become a critical part of the business for actually accomplishing business tasks. Project management in other areas, such as construction; have long followed the same basic principles.

The skills of organization, time management, delegation, and communications are indeed transferable to business situations. In fact, the following principles hold true no matter what effort is undertaken. They are not limited to, nor in many cases do they even mention implementation or software development activities.

Bing, (1994)[1] describes eight "Principles of Successful Projects" based on his extensive practical experience in the field as follows:

❖   "There must be a project as defined in the PMBOK (Project Management Book of Knowledge), and not just a task or an ongoing activity.

❖   There must be a single leader (project manager), who is experienced and willing to take the responsibility for the work.

- ❖   There must be an informed and supportive management that delegates appropriate authority to
  the project manager.

- ❖   There must be a dedicated team of qualified people to do the work of the project.

- ❖   The project goal must be clearly defined along
  with priorities of the 'shareholders.'

- ❖   There must be an integrated plan that outlines
  the action required in order to reach the goal.

- ❖   There must be a schedule establishing the time
  goals of the project.

- ❖   There must be a budget of costs and/or resources required for the project."

These eight principles extend beyond just information systems implementations and apply to all types of
projects. There is also much other literature written about
generic project management that can be applied to software package implementation projects. Good solid project
management is a cornerstone of success, whether it is implementation of software or other business projects.

Another reason for this book is to bring order to the
chaos of the installation process and transform it into a
true and successful implementation methodology. Many,
like McNurlin and Sprague have come to realize that[2], "As
much as possible these days, companies prefer to buy a
package rather than to build the application in-house."

Now is the time to assimilate good business practices and good project management processes into the
methodologies of implementation. My methodology gleans
successful practices from both business and IT worlds and

melds them together in a comprehensive methodology that provides a solid foundation for repeatable success.

A solid methodology, supported by an experienced Program Management Office (PMO) can garner enough management backing to provide necessary funding, an environment capable of accepting change, and adequate staffing with adequate time to support the fundamental elements necessary to provide a foundation for success.

A project attempted to be implemented in an unreasonable time frame, with insufficient budget, or with inadequate software will always be unsuccessful.

To Plan or not to Plan

Planning provides for measurements and can provide an indicator of probable success, but planning alone will not determine the success or failure of a project. No one bit or piece of any methodology can guarantee success.

Do you remember the fallacy that an infinite number of monkeys sitting at keyboards could eventually recreate the bible? Even an infinite budget will not guarantee success by itself. The increased dollars may make some team members happy, but will not guarantee success.

There are also many important pieces to the package software implementation process. Each process has its place in the implementation lifecycle and none can be so critical as to singularly guarantee success in the absence of others.

Dealing with Change

It is difficult for individuals to deal with change, even a little change. However, as above, planning and re-planning is and must be a way of life for the project manager. Re-planning by definition means change, so change must be a way of life for the PMO or project manager. To paraphrase a popular bumper sticker, "Change Happens."

Among the prime responsibilities of the PMO is to accept change, embrace change, advocate change, instigate change, react to change, and even incite change in the team and the organization.

As Peter Senge, in 1995, so elegantly states,[3] "If there is one single thing a learning organization does well, it is helping people embrace change. People in learning organization react more quickly when their environment changes because they know how to anticipate changes when they occur and how to create kinds of changes they want. Change and learning may not exactly be synonymous, however they are inextricably connected." Learning organizations are more adaptable to change and will embrace it before others and some organizations are more amenable to change than others.

> *Among the prime responsibilities of the PMO is to accept change, embrace change, advocate change, instigate change, react to change, and even incite change in the team and the organization.*

Those in the information technology profession deal with change every day. It is part of their job to assist others to make, and embrace change. It is in their best interest to deal with change as a learning experience and to make change a part of the process.

It's interesting to note that many IT professionals themselves are reluctant to change. This conundrum can be overcome by education, group effort, and peer pressure.

The bottom line is that change comes naturally to a learning organization and with an organization used to changing; learning is a byproduct of that change process. Project success is a result of positive change.

However, since many implementations are conducted in non-IT and non-learning organizations it becomes mandatory for the PMO and project teams to become the champions of the change process.

What's Past is Prologue

Since few of the major consultant implementation methodologies were developed specifically for package implementation, consultants and others have been forced to extract bits and pieces from current methodologies and manipulate these steps in order to make them fit each individual situation.

Indeed, many of the waves, phases, milestones, and steps built for software development and implementation also fit the application software implementation process.

Methodologies are not like recipes that can be exactly followed.

No methodology should be blindly followed.

However, significant differences do exist and no methodology should be blindly followed. Methodologies are not like recipes that can be exactly followed. People and culture are two ingredients that must be adapted to during each implementation.

The use of expensive and hard-to-find information technology personnel during a package software implementation is reduced by as much as two thirds vs. a software development and implementation effort.

During the package software implementation process, users are encouraged to be involved much earlier during the process. User file building begins almost immediately upon beginning the project as the base software structure is already built to accept data.

Early user involvement is a bonus for the PMO. As evidence of the value of user involvement early in the process, Saleem, (1996)[4] says, "The benefits of collaborating will be evident in the litmus test of any software project: user acceptance. Research shows that users with a high degree of participation in system development will demonstrate greater system acceptance than the users with a low degree of participation."

Many companies and significant portions of industries have found it useful and advantageous to implement software packages as opposed to self-developed software. Time-to-value is significant among the reasons to use package software rather than developing applications from scratch. Software packages can be up and running in significantly less time and with much less organizational trauma, than self developed applications.

History proves that active management involvement as well as following a proven methodology are crucial to the success of a project.

Testing, the bane of development projects is also greatly reduced during the implementation of software packages. Many rounds of testing will have already occurred during the software build development process. This does not eliminate the need for further testing, but reduces the amount of time dedicated to testing.

Successful implementation of package software can and does occur more often than some literature would suggest. Much literature does not specifically address package software implementation, but rather it describes system development and its associated implementation. This translates to reported project failure rates being highly weighted toward software development and implementation.

History proves that active management involvement as well as following a proven methodology are crucial to the success of a project.

Planning is one of the most important aspects of a successful implementation and software must work, at least substantially as advertised, in order to be implemented as intended.

Another Fine Mess . . .

Oliver Hardy used to delight in reminding Stan Laurel that he had just landed them in "another fine mess." So too, we must be reminded that billions of dollars are spent for the design and development of package software. Organizations spend hundreds of millions of dollars annually on the process of trying to make software work in their unique circumstances. They expect benefit from their investment and those in the consulting and implementation business keep landing them in "another fine mess."

"More than 80 percent of IT-related projects are late, over budget, lacking in functionality, or never delivered."

In a healthcare setting, lives depend on the results of successful package software implementation. In other situations, the very success or failure of the business may depend upon successful or unsuccessful software implementation. This has become even more acutely true in the current e-business environment.

The significance of the need for a viable methodology with its imbedded processes is evidenced by a review of literature, which provides a pattern of project failures caused by an unwillingness, ambivalence, or ignorance toward following successful methodologies.

Good News and Bad News

Julia King[5] says, "Information systems project management is worse than awful, and it is costing companies more than $100 billion annually. That's the good news.

The bad news is that a majority of companies remain incapable of or unwilling to make even modest changes that could slash development costs by millions of dollars each month. Moreover, poor project planning and management are to blame for companies scrapping almost a third of new software projects for a loss of $80 billion annually."

Late to Mitigate

"More than 80 percent of IT-related projects are late, over budget, lacking in functionality, or never delivered. Many of those at risk could be identified at the start. By using a simple checklist and either tenaciously pursuing the completion of the outstanding items or putting in place risk mitigation steps to counter the residual risk, many of those projects would be successful.[6]"

One way to determine if a project is in a fine mess or headed toward success or failure is to ask random team members the following questions:

❖ What is the purpose of this project?

❖ What is your role in this project?

❖   What are the two greatest impediments to the success of this project?

❖   What two good things you can say about this project?

❖   What two bad things you can say about this project?

❖   Who is your customer?

❖   Will this project be a success?

Compare the answers to the published documentation, org chart, and status reports. You may also wish to save the answers with lessons learned. Never miss an opportunity to acquire knowledge from others; it will broaden your own horizons.

Lack of Communications

Lack of communications can be blamed for many ills in personal life, the business world, and project management.

> *Never miss an opportunity to acquire knowledge from others; it will broaden your own horizons.*

One writer, Sullivan (2000)[7] says, "In studying why projects fail, the number one reason is poor communications. Lack of understanding by the participants regarding what is expected of them by the project manager causes more projects to sink than any other."

Lack of Skills

Booth, (2000)[8] conducted a research study among 1,375 IT professionals, including IT managers, IT consultants, and IT implementers. Results showed that 40% of projects fail to meet the business requirements. A summary of key findings showed reasons for failure included:

❖ "The broad base of project-responsible workers is not adequately skilled

❖ Project-responsible workers are key contributors to project failure and management's de-valuation of the PM job role

❖ Business and leadership skills are critical success factors in the high-stakes world of IT."

The findings also indicated that furthering project-management training and creating a project oversight group or program management office (PMO) is associated with lower failure rates.

"50% of programs take longer than expected and 60% of programs cost more than expected."

In addition, the same study revealed that sixty percent of organizations don't offer such training, and 61 percent of firms don't have an oversight group in place to be sure the portfolio of projects is on course for success or terminated responsibly. It goes on to show that 50% of programs take longer than expected and 60% of programs cost more than expected.

More Project Failures

In a 1994 study[9] conducted of 8,000 projects, only 16% met original time and budget estimates. The five reasons listed for project failure included:

❖ "Lack of user input

❖ Incomplete requirements

❖   Changing requirements and specifications

❖   Lack of executive support

❖   Lack of technical skills."

Three sides to every story

Most projects have a specific finish date, budget, and scope. This trio of time, money, and scope (which is defined as the combination of all project goals and tasks, and the work required to complete them) is often referred to as the "project triangle". If you adjust any one of these elements, the other two are affected. While all three elements are important, typically one will have the most influence during any given project.

I like to offer a choice; you can have it fast, cheap, or good, pick any two. For instance, if you choose to have it fast and cheap, quality will suffer. If you choose to have it good and fast, the price will increase significantly.

Scope Creep

Scope creep is probably mentioned as one of the causes of project overruns or failures more than any other cause. Scope control consumes a major part of project management activities on a daily basis. Among the reasons for this is that, as a project progresses, team members learn more about the business and users learn more about the features and functions of the software being implemented. As a result, they tend to find new uses for the system or want to change newly discovered processes.

Other reasons for scope creep include lack of a detail plan to follow and lack of an appropriate change management process.

Just Because

Because many of the preceding detrimental activities are self inflicted, they do not have to continue to disrupt projects. The methodology described in later chapters conveys an organized collection and sequence of phases, milestones, and steps along with the surrounding business management and project management practices that have proven to be affective for the implementation of package software. It details deliverables required for successful implementations and provides examples for each phase in the process.

Project management tips, risk management techniques and quality assurance practices are covered at length to provide mitigation criteria should the implementation process begin to stray off its intended course. Program Management Office duties and responsibilities are outlined in detail.

Processes leading toward a successful implementation can be summed up in three words: Plan, Do, Review.

Project deliverables are outlined with sufficient detail to be used for actual projects. Documents from successful projects are described as examples with sufficient background provided to be useful for the novice as well as the experienced project manager.

The preceding findings from various sources are taken into account. Valid project management techniques and steps are outlined to mitigate these and other causes for project failure. The result is a practical hybrid methodology developed from research, surveys, and practical experience.

The Elephant

One of the largest and most respected institutions in the field of project management is the Project Management Institute (PMI). A quote from the Project Management Institute Book of Knowledge (1999),[10] "Project management is a relatively young profession and while there is substantial commonality around what is done, there is relatively little commonality in the terms used" confirms not only that the elephant is large, but it is also hard to describe.

Many of the methodologies studied show some similarity in what is said but not necessarily how it is said. Some are verbose but miss the key points and some are succinct but miss critical details necessary to conduct successful implementations.

There are at least as many terms for the various phases and steps of a package implementation project as there are writers extolling their own particular methodology.

Regardless of terminology, the processes and procedures leading toward a successful implementation are relatively straightforward and can be summed up in three words: Plan, Do, Review.

The Mouse

Small amounts of data are found that actually review the successes and failures from package software implementations. Much available data supports the development and implementation of developed software rather than specific implementation of package software. However, there are similarities and my survey results generally support other literature findings from developed software findings.

The process of implementing package software is not so unique as to preclude the process of sound project management techniques applied to a specific set of circumstances, in this case commercial package software implementation for an organization.

The rules of project management are extended by the application of those steps, features, and functions idiosyncratic to package software implementation projects and how to achieve its ultimate successful assimilation of the package software into the day-to-day operations of an organization.

Surveys

Two surveys conducted almost a year apart were developed and sent to vendors, consultants, and users who had been or were currently involved in package software implementations at the time of the survey. All respondents had been involved in multiple implementations and some had been conducting implementations in various roles for more than twenty years.

Lack of a plan is the number one reason contributing to project failure.

The following list presents an overview of significant findings, but is not in order of significance or priority.

* ❖ If you define your requirements up front, develop, follow, and regularly measure against a work plan, obtain management support, and communicate with the team, chances of a successful project are dramatically increased.

* ❖ There are few elements which can substantially increase the odds of project success, but there are many things which can cause project failure.

❖   You can never test too much or too often.

❖   Successful projects have a defined beginning and end.

❖   A project without a work plan will fail almost twice as often as not.

❖   The vast majority of projects have limited resources.

❖   Most projects have specific time constraints.

❖   Projects should be broken down into manageable phases, each with specific deliverables.

❖   Project phases should be concluded with a review and approval of the deliverables for that phase.

❖   Design of a final deliverable is limited to the capability of the application software and the skills of the team to take advantage of its functions.

❖   Projects involving packaged software have limited flexibility in adapting the application to the way business is conducted.

❖   Package implementation projects involve changing behaviors in the organization.

❖   The culture of an organization can positively or negatively affect the final project outcome and should not be ignored.

❖   Leading and managing are different skills, both are required for project success.

- ❖ People are led, projects are managed.

- ❖ Risk management is imperative for a successful project outcome.

- ❖ Actions in one area of a project will likely affect another area of the project.

- ❖ If an interface works once, it is not an indicator that it will work with other conditions.

- ❖ A stable system environment is required for valid test results.

- ❖ There will never be enough time or resources to test an application under all conditions.

- ❖ Change control is necessary to maintain project scope.

- ❖ Business processes must be understood by the implementation team.

- ❖ The more complex a project the more essential it is to have a qualified team.

- ❖ All documents (electronic and paper) produced during a project must be dated.

- ❖ In a project work plan, team accountability means no accountability.

- ❖ Increases in project scope decrease chances for successful outcomes.

- ❖ Successful projects do not end on the day of cut-over.

❖   Lessons learned from each implementation are valuable instructions for the future, and should be maintained and widely distributed.

❖   Each implementation project is unique, but shares many similar characteristics with other implementation projects.

While there is no single factor which can create a guarantee of project success, the development and regular use of work plan emerges as close to the ideal candidate.

There are physical, budget, or environmental limits placed on all projects. In addition, multiple projects share requirements for budget and compete for time and resources normally devoted to other business tasks.

Experience and research shows that there are verifiable and quantifiable causes of implementation project success which can be applied to any project in order to increase the propensity for success. Similarly, tools alone cannot guarantee implementation project success. They must be used in conjunction with sound management practices.

Project success is only achieved with an amalgam of knowledge, skills, abilities, and tools, blended with appropriate resources and management/user support then liberally mixed with appropriate amounts of communication.

> *Success is only achieved with an amalgam of knowledge, skills, abilities, and tools, blended with appropriate resources and management support.*

Chapter Two -
The Case for Project Management

Leadership and management of the process for implementing package software must be organized, and objective. Project planning should involve discreet steps and begin during the purchasing cycle.

Much has been written about the factors which lead to project success, but regardless of their individual value, each project requires a focal point and that focal point is the project manager.

Project management has slowly evolved into a unique discipline. However, the complexity of the modern business environment has dictated increased speed to value. Businesses are not afforded the luxury of individual projects finishing before other projects are begun. This rapidity of change has spawned a new era of project management requiring managing and leading multiple concurrent projects. Thus the Program Management Office has emerged.

Skill can overcome lack of tools, but no tool can compensate for lack of skills.

PMO leaders must be skilled and educated. They must possess inherent abilities to lead under duress as well as understand and communicate at any level in an organization. They must be born leaders and schooled tacticians with appropriate tools at their disposal and resources at the ready.

One definition of project management offered by Kyle, (1998)[11] states "Specifically, project management is the art of directing and coordinating human and material resources throughout the life of a project, by using modern management techniques to achieve pre-determined objectives of scope, quality, time, cost, and participant satisfaction."

Michael Greer, (1999)[12] states that "project manager responsibility must be matched by equivalent authority." A project manager without authority is like an automobile with everything but an engine, fully capable of locomotion, but no means of propulsion."

Gartner, (2000)[13] predicted that, "Through 2004, IT organizations that establish enterprise standards for project management, including a project office with suitable governance, will experience half the major project cost overruns, delays, and cancellations of those that fail to do so."

While project and program management are proven factors for success, it is also important to note that inappropriate choices can contribute to failure. Trepper, (2000)[14] says, "Nothing derails an IT development project faster than sloppy project management."

Project Methodologies

The project methodology defines the rules for management, co-ordination, and completion of a project. It begins with planning and includes managing quality and risk for a project. The need for an integrated methodology within an organization accentuates the need for integrated project management, such as a Program Management Office.

"A *methodology* is a set of guidelines or principles that can be tailored and applied to a specific situation. In a project environment, these guidelines might be a list of things to do. A methodology could also be a specific approach, templates, forms, and even checklists used over the project life cycle. A formal project methodology should lead the work of all team members throughout the life cycle of a project, but it may be useful to think about what a project management methodology is not: a quick fix; a silver bullet; a temporary solution; or a cookbook approach for project success.[15]"

Many vendors, consultants, and professional services firms have their own version of a methodology. Each contains phases, milestones, and steps for completion. Although they differ in terminology and style, they all contain certain basic stages or phases. Some elaborate the number of phases or stages in great detail and rhetoric while others minimize them to as few as four to six.

A methodology developed by the UK Government, (1989)[16] named for Projects In Controlled Environments (PRINCE), is a structured methodology with a standard approach to the management of projects. It is still in use today and it enables projects to have:

❖ "A controlled and organized start, middle and end

❖ Regular reviews of progress against plan and against the business case

❖ Flexible decision points

❖ Automatic management control of any deviations from the plan

❖ Involvement of management and stakeholders at the right time and place during the project

❖ Good communication channels between the project, project management, and the rest of the organization."

There are numerous other methodologies, each purporting to solve problems and contribute to success. Many have been relegated to shelfware status due to their enormous bulk.

To be successful, a methodology must be practical and nimble. It must contain enough of a roadmap to guide, but must be flexible enough to allow for change of directions as dictated by circumstances and culture. Above all, a usable methodology must be simple enough to be easily understood. It can be complex, but not complicated.

"Over the years, even those involved in managing projects have observed that projects have common characteristics that can be formalized into a structural process, which allows them to manage projects more effectively.

Each phase can typically be brought to closure in some logical way before the next project phase begins; and each phase results in discrete milestones or deliverables, which provide the starting point for the next phase. Cost and schedule estimates, plans, requirements, and specifications should be updated and evaluated at the end of each phase. . .[17]"

A PMO must choose a methodology and standards for the particular project at hand and stick to them. The methodology and standards must be consistent and consistently applied throughout the project. The methodology must be understood and accepted by all members of the team at the beginning of the project so all have a common understanding and begin with a solid foundation.

Software development and software package implementations may share a majority of phases but they remain sufficiently different to obviate complete interchangeability.

Parts is Parts

However one chooses to describe the various parts of a methodology, as waves, phases, or stages, none of the following elements of implementation can be eliminated and produce successful results from a project. At the most base level they are:

- ❖ Planning

- ❖ Execution

- ❖ Closure.

Planning begins with an idea or unfulfilled need and proceeds through to the development, evaluation, documentation of a business case, and acceptance. Planning for an implementation includes more than just building a work plan, it includes defining the project purpose, defining scope, and building all of the elements included in a project charter document, such as described later.

Project planning is necessary for resource allocation and execution of project activities. It includes development of the overall project structure and work plan that will form the foundation of the project management process throughout the project lifecycle. Planning also includes resource and budget allocation, tools selection and education, a project charter document, and a work plan.

During execution, project activities defined in the charter and work plan are tracked, measured, and completed. The project execution stage includes execution of planned activities and the testing, training, and ultimate productive use of the system. It also includes change, risk, and quality management processes.

There should be a formal process for closing a project, which by definition has a beginning and an end. This includes evaluating the successful and unsuccessful aspects of the project.

Closing a project is not equivalent to Go-Live or turn over to operations. Closing includes a post-implementation review.

According to Davis, (1998)[18], "After users have become comfortable with the use of the system (generally three to six months after activation), a post-implementation review of the system should be conducted. This review should include system design, documentation, and adequacy of hardware, procedure compliance, and user satisfaction."

> Projects are like moving cars, if you want to steer, you have to get on the inside and grab the wheel.

A post-implementation review should also include identifying opportunities for improvement that can be leveraged in future projects, evaluating the performance of the methodology and tools, determination of needs for additional training, and performance reviews for project leadership and individual team members.

Successful program and project management at the highest level should provide for leadership, management and user involvement, a controlled but flexible environment, and good communications. All of which are essential ingredients for success.

Organization of a Project

The same system is never implemented in the same way as it had been implemented before. In fact, organizations usually change their mind regarding implementation during the implementation process itself. Indeed, numerous projects are so loosely organized that they lead to frustration at best and failure at worst.

There is clearly a need for change in the way projects are organized and run. Fitzgerald, (1998)[19] states, "Because of much publicity for spectacular software implementation project failures, companies have become more wary of new software implementation. The fear is that it will not come up on time, will not work as expected, and that it will cost much more than originally planned or budgeted for. As a result, projects are receiving more scrutiny with increased need for bottom line return."

Reduced cycle time for software development and enhancement, changing market conditions, and repeated failures have only continued the scrutiny by which projects and programs are measured. Increased planning has only recently begun to receive the resources and time necessary to achieve a proclivity for project success.

One of the goals of project planning is to define scope and integrate all project activities into a coordinated whole. Properly defined scope, sensitive project management, performance monitoring, and personal responsibility will still not guarantee a successful project. Each implementation is unique with its own singular personality. Each has its own culture, team members, sponsors, and stakeholders. Each has its own budget restrictions, time limits, and other constraints.

ISO Annex A., (1995)[20] agrees and states that, "No two projects are the same. Variations in organizational policies and procedures, acquisition methods and strategies, project size and complexity, system requirements, and development methods, among other things, influence how a system is acquired, developed, operated, or maintained."

These statements lend credence to the fact that each project is unique and must be dealt with uniquely. A successful methodology therefore, allows for uniqueness of circumstance and changes in the processes with which a project is planned for and executed. Stated it another way, a successful methodology allows for flexibility in execution.

PMO vs. Project Manager

> *Each project is unique and must be dealt with uniquely.*

There is a distinction between a project manager and a Program Management Office. Project managers are responsible for planning, tracking, managing, and controlling individual projects. The PMO is responsible for planning, tracking, managing, and controlling either individual or more commonly, multiple projects. The position taken herein is that the terms Project Management Office and Program Management Office are used interchangeably and will be considered synonymous with project management unless specifically noted otherwise.

The term Program, and thus Program Management Office, refers to a project or set of projects (related or not) that need to be managed in a coordinated manner in order to achieve results that would not otherwise be attained. Although individual projects may or may not share resources, a PMO structure dictates that projects with or without shared resources be managed in a coordinated manner.

Project Requirements

All projects, by definition must have a beginning and an end. It is important to define and put in writing what constitutes the beginning and end of a project so all team members, stakeholders, sponsors, and champions will know when to begin and when they are finished. By developing requirements for the project, the team can begin to define where the project begins and ends.

Requirements are useful only if they are followed and a project is a success only if the requirements have been effectively met. Herzlich, (1994)[21] relates that, "The project requirements are an intermediate step between the project objective and its implementation. The requirements should be based on the original definition and include the processes for achieving a successful end of project."

In other words, no matter how well planned a project is, it will fail if it is not executed to achieve the project requirements. The execution process and related deliverables must be monitored and measured during the course of and at the end of the project.

Part B -
The Science

Chapter Three -
Evolving from Art to Science

Project implementation of package software can evolve from an art to a science, if the appropriate tools, techniques, and resources are utilized. Project planning is an iterative process and while many projects fail, the majority of project failure causes are preventable.

Appropriate tools, techniques, and resources can greatly increase the propensity for project success. Sound, replicable, and positive project management practices for the implementation process of package software can be accomplished. Success is indeed repeatable with appropriate leadership and tools.

My experience and research shows that known methodologies, principles, and practices support the following statements:

❖ Certain basic elements of project management can reduce project risks and increase the potential for project success

❖ Development and regular use of a project work plan, especially one built without a predetermined end date, is an important factor contributing to project success

❖ Ongoing communications is an important aspect of successful implementation

❖ Project management can not remain a static process and continue to be successful

❖ Successful methodologies should be designed to be followed situationally

❖   Knowledge of all circumstances surrounding a package software application implementation process can never be known

❖   An effective methodology should be adaptable to a wide variety of people, processes, and technology

❖   Software should work, at least substantially as advertised, in order to be implemented as intended

❖   Software package implementation projects should consist of 80% people and process, and 20% technology

❖   Project tasks should be delegated to the lowest level capable of handling them.

Research can never be complete regarding this topic as people and technology, two essential ingredients, are constantly in a state of change. However, we can and must improve upon the current project management processes.

Causes of Project Success

Each implementation project is unique, but shares many similar characteristics with other implementation projects.

Projects, by their very nature, have a beginning and end. There are physical, budget, and environmental limits placed on all projects. Projects share requirements for budget and compete for time and resources with other projects and normal business tasks.

Given those high level similarities, there are various potential causes of implementation project success which can be applied to all projects in order to increase the potential for success.

While there is no single factor, which can create a guarantee of project success, the development and regular use of work plan does come close to the ideal candidate.

Tools, methods, and processes alone cannot guarantee implementation project success. They must be used in conjunction with sound management practices and receive management support, budget, and time to accomplish the required tasks.

Tom's Tenets for project success

Analyzing the vastness of data provides compelling tenets for project success and failure. A representative list of project success tenets form the foundation for the methodology and operating principles.

❖   Quality input equals quality output.

❖   Initial planning and preparation should be completed before project work activity commences.

❖   Planning, preparation, completeness, and accuracy are essential to an effective charter.

❖   A charter is a contract for success and as such, should be understood and agreed to by all parties.

❖   Proper planning produces effective and efficient projects.

❖   Methodologies provide necessary structure to implementation projects.

❖   A single leader or point of authority for any project, is essential.

❖   Executive management knowledge, buy in, and open support is required.

❖   User involvement at all levels is necessary.

❖   Technology is a tool, not a solution.

❖   Change management is an integral part of project success.

❖   Realistic expectations lead to clear requirements and vice versa.

❖   Risk management by its nature, reduces project risks.

❖   Adequate resources meet reasonable dates.

❖   A work plan, if used properly, can be one of the most important tools for project success.

❖   Change control provides intended results.

❖   Effective training leads to improved system adoption.

❖   Unstated elegance should never drive unnecessary tasks.

❖   The cut-over process has a life of its own and should be treated with dignity.

❖   True success is not measured only on the day of cut-over.

❖   Post implementation processes solidify success and increase system assimilation.

Tom's Tenets for project failure

The following project failure tenets highlight activities or processes that singularly or collectively, can and usually do lead to implementation project failure. Failure is an educator equal to success. The following tenets, together with those above solidify the foundation for the methodology and operating principles.

❖   Without a definition of success, the only alternative is failure.

❖   Failure to plan means planning for failure.

❖   Work not defined in detail will yield an inadequate plan.

❖   An unused work plan is unspent success.

❖   Poor participation from the project Sponsor is a harbinger of problems to follow.

❖   Insufficient user involvement results in insufficient system value.

❖   Lack of quality is a symptom of project failure.

❖   A project without a leader is like a boat without a rudder.

❖   Poor project leadership will directly lead to poor project results.

❖   Uncontrolled changes directly correlate to an end date in motion.

❖   Inadequate resources lead to unanticipated results.

❖   Unregulated changes provide undesirable deliverables.

❖   Increases in project scope are inversely proportional to project success.

❖   Unrealistic objectives provide undesirable results.

❖   An unused charter is an unused resource.

❖   Missed milestones, like missed heart beats, cause project arrhythmia.

❖   Risk management is inversely proportional to project risk.

❖   Parsimonious budgets steal from project success.

❖   Unrealistic time frames lead to missed deadlines.

❖   Undocumented systems document failure.

❖   Inadequate testing yields unpredictable results.

❖   Resources added late in the project are not equal to resources added early.

❖   Lack of, or ineffective training will lead to lack of, or ineffective use of the system.

❖   Inadequate software is inadequate.

❖   A predefined end date without adequate input is
       like a predefined cooking time without knowledge
       of the ingredients.

❖   Failure does not occur on the day of cut-over.

❖   Project success is fleeting but project failure re-
       mains.

The preceding tenets for success and failure help
define the functional underpinnings of projects. These
tenets provide a perspective for project planning, execution, and delivery. They are equally useful when beginning
a project and for assigning roles and responsibilities.

A review of the preceding tenets only
at the end of a project will yield more examples of failure. Project planning must be
proactive, not reactive.

*Project plan-
ning must be
proactive, not
reactive.*

Planning - The First Question

A question to consider when planning for a software
package implementation project, is, "How do I eat an elephant?" The answer is, "One bite at a time." This simple
question and its answer can have a profound affect when
applied to implementation projects.

Project management practices which follow this formula for breaking a project down into manageable steps
will increase chances of project success.

The process of successfully breaking a project into
smaller "bite size" pieces and managing those pieces includes:

❖   Construction of intermediate milestones and
deadlines to measure progress early and often

❖   Creation of a minimum and maximum allowable
time limit for all tasks

❖   Development of metrics to measure progress and
success

❖   Documenting and celebration of small successes
along the way.

Maintain an overall perspective toward tasks so that
the work plan tasks are not made so small as to create a
self defeating process. This means that the PMO should
also watch the minimum time limit on tasks. A task scheduled to last a few hours or less for instance, may consume
more time to maintain, track, and measure than the time
necessary to actually perform the work.

Planning - The Second Question

The second question to ask when planning for a project is, "How will I know when we are finished." Many projects continue on past their useful life cycle due to a lack
of specific planning, including detail steps for close-out.

The planning process should include the details and
criteria for efficiently and effectively ending a project. It
should contain specific steps to aid the process. In addition, specific deliverables should be described, such that
their completion will contribute to signal acceptance and
the end of the project.

Implications of the preceding two questions and answers regarding the principles and practices of implementation project management indicate that proper and organ-

ized planning along with effective communications can reduce project failures usually attributed to other causes.

A final, complete, and all encompassing methodology can not be developed because the process of implementation involves people, technology, and circumstances which do not remain static. Situations differ from product to product, team to team, and company to company. People have built-in biases based on life experiences which distinctly differ from one to another.

Although no single process, plan, or methodology can solve all problems, the following methodology attempts to glean the currently known and proven best practices. It includes tools, tips, techniques, and process descriptions to minimize activities which have shown to be indicators leading to project failure and includes those activities and tools which have proven to be indicators leading to project success.

Chapter Four -
Roles and Responsibilities

Implementation Leadership Roles and Responsibilities

An effective PMO has proven to positively influence project success. Light, (2000)[22] says, "The [recent] success of the many project offices that addressed the year 2000 problem has proven the project office to be a 'best practice' for delivering successful projects. . . The roles and skills of a project office, plus support for a consistent and disciplined approach to chartering, prioritizing, and resourcing project work with attention to quality and project knowledge collection, can help mitigate these risks."

Project management and the Program Management Office in particular, should be based on the following principles:

❖ Projects should be based on business need and focused on business objectives

❖ Requirements are the basis for defining work and measuring quality

❖ Priorities are managed through use of a project plan

❖ Projects should move an organization toward an improved state

❖ Estimates should always be based on facts

❖   Resource productivity is leveraged through the use of a methodology, training, tools, techniques, and the reuse of knowledge

❖   Risk mitigation is an integral part of project management

❖   Measure early and measure often.

The following summarizes various implementation project management roles and responsibilities. Roles and responsibilities are outlined for the three main leadership and management functions of implementation project management. It begins with the highest level of management, the Steering Committee, progresses to the Project Sponsor, and to the PMO.

Role of the Steering Committee

A Steering Committee ensures that implementation projects are consistent with business plans. Integration, management of current technologies, and ubiquitous data access require adoption and enforcement of standards.

The Steering Committee should be responsible for enforcement of standards for project management, quality assurance, and ongoing administration. It should be senior level management team representing a diverse cross section of the business.

Composition of the Committee should include executive and senior managers from across the enterprise. It should have sufficient authority and represent all significant operating entities.

The PMO is usually an ex-officio member of the Steering Committee for the duration of major projects. The reason for the ex-officio membership status is to maintain a voice in the process while preventing a potential conflict of interest vote.

The following describes typical high level responsibilities.

Steering Committee Responsibilities

The responsibilities of the Steering Committee include:

- ❖ Direct overall strategy formulation

- ❖ Review program and project activities

- ❖ Set overall priorities

- ❖ Review summary project plans

- ❖ Review resource assignments

- ❖ Provide advice and counsel regarding key business and project issues

- ❖ Review and approve key deliverables

- ❖ Monitor overall progress and resolve significant conflicts

- ❖ Review project changes that have an organization-wide impact

- ❖ Resolve significant management issues

- ❖ Monitor project adherence to organization-wide objectives

❖   Act as advocate for project implementation efforts

❖   Maintain active communication with the Project
Sponsor, teams, PMO, and project stakeholders.

Evaluation of major project proposals which support
strategic business goals and initiatives is also a role of the
Committee.

Strategic planning and design oversight should be
dynamic and flexible to provide for changes in business
mission, vision, goals, and objectives.

Budget Approval and Resource Commitment

The committee should not be a replacement for the
ongoing business budget processes, but should work with
the Project Sponsor and PMO to maintain an adequate
funding level for an implementation project.

Commitment of resources, including both staffing
and funding, should be reconciled with the resource requirements of other business activities and overall budget
constraints.

The committee should periodically review benefits,
performance, and return on investment from projects. It
should also review new projects and changes to existing
projects to ensure enterprise-wide consistency.

Project Sponsor Responsibilities

A Project Sponsor should provide guidance to the
PMO and project teams. The Sponsor should also assist
to resolve project issues affecting departmental policies.
Reviewing security and privacy policies related to the use

of and access to enterprise-wide information are also part of the duties.

The person fulfilling this role is usually a management team member who can operate across business units and the enterprise. The Sponsor should command sufficient authority, respect, and influence to be effective and must be found higher in the organization than from a single department.

Sponsors are responsible for ensuring that projects support the enterprise business goals throughout their life cycle, ensuring that projects stay on schedule and within budget, and also ensuring effort is applied to solve issues that require senior management attention.

Edward Ziv, (2000)[23] morosely says, "Without one, the project will be guillotined at a budget meeting, or your resources will continue to be borrowed until the project dies."

The PMO communicates more often with the Project Sponsor, who has a more active role in the project than with the Steering Committee. However, Project Sponsors are usually members of Steering Committees.

Benefits realization measurement and review as well as critical success factors measurement and review are also duties of the Project Sponsor in conjunction with the PMO. To be truly successful and perceived as such, a project must not only be successful by subjective means, it must be objectively successful.

> To be truly successful and perceived as such, a project must not only be successful by subjective means, it must be objectively successful.

The Project Sponsor:

❖   Provides advice and counsel regarding policy, direction, scope, and level of detail dealing with major business issues

❖   Removes barriers to progress

❖   Ensures that adequate resources are available to the PMO

❖   Ensures that key deliverables are reviewed before presentation to the Steering Committee

❖   Monitors progress and assists to resolve project issues

❖   Keeps executive management informed on a regular basis

❖   Serves as a conduit for enterprise-wide departmental input to a project

❖   Acts as a member of the Steering Committee

❖   Acts as program advocate

❖   Maintains communication with teams and acts upon their recommendations.

Sponsors usually are selected from executive leadership and should ensure a project stays on schedule, within budget, and work to resolve issues requiring management attention.

Role of the Program Management Office

The PMO, and project managers, should possess and demonstrate knowledge, skills, and abilities in many disciplines, including technical, managerial, and business. Anyone filling these roles should maintain a very high level of personal integrity and be capable of leading, motivating, teaching, and training. Some of the skills and abilities required to thrive in this role can be learned and some must be innate.

As Levine, (2001)[24] so eloquently states, "Obviously, we cannot take it for granted that any senior person or even any manager will have the skills and temperament for project management. Some of these skills can be learned, but many important qualifications are embedded in a person's personality."

> A project manager should maintain a very high level of personal integrity and be capable of leading, motivating, teaching, and training.

Melymuka, (2000)[25] also agrees, "You can train somebody to be a good project manager, but great project managers seem to be born, not made. Excellence depends on certain innate characteristics: Some of us got 'em, and some of us don't."

Knowledge can be developed or learned through experience, study, or investigation. Ability is the innate potential to perform mental and physical actions. Skills are the result of repeatedly applying knowledge and exercising abilities.

A PMO should provide detail project guidance regarding policy, direction, risk, and scope. It should remove major barriers to progress and ensure adequate resources and funding are being allocated. Additional responsibilities include reviewing deliverables, measuring progress, and providing regular and frequent communications and progress reports to all project stakeholders.

One of the first things to understand regarding project management is that interpersonal communication should be a way of life for the PMO. As Covey, (1998)[26] puts it, "To be understood, you must seek to understand."

An effective PMO must first understand the environment, the proposed technology, the task at hand, the tools available, risks, limits, and constraints, and the people to be involved. If the PMO does not understand the environment, resources, and stakeholders involved, it is impossible to promulgate the intentions of management to the team.

Project management requires a set of tools and techniques used to produce deliverables that will accomplish the objective and satisfy the customer as well as to ensure that all stakeholders and team members have a voice in the process. These tools assist the PMO to minimize risk, complete the project on time within budget, and with deliverables of the quality expected.

The Canadian Government, (1997)[27] agrees with the same basic principles as other authorities, including the fact that *there is a clear need for a PMO* and the PMO:

❖   "Is responsible for oversight and management of a project

❖   Is responsible to have and follow a formal methodology

❖   Is responsible for risk management

❖ Is responsible for scope management and the change management process

❖ Is responsible for project deliverables

❖ Is a leader and facilitator

❖ Is responsible for the progress and outcomes of the project

❖ Works as liaison with the Project Sponsor

❖ Is responsible for project communication

❖ Is responsible to teach and train team members

❖ Is responsible for budget management

❖ Is responsible for resource management."

Although the fulcrum upon which the results of a project rest is the PMO, success or failure still belongs to the whole team. It is rare that an implementation project is a one person team and so it is obvious that there is a need for a leader. Someone must be accountable for the desired outcome and this responsibility rests with the PMO.

In the past, the role of the Project Manager has been more limited in scope and function than current situations dictate. Literature supports both the traditional and the new role with expanded duties for the Project Manager, now often the PMO.

> *Although the fulcrum upon which the results of a project rest is the PMO, success or failure still belongs to the whole team.*

As Belzer, (2001)[28] states, "Just as there is a fine line between programs and projects, the program manager's role overlaps with but differs from functional management and project management in important ways. Program management requires project management and functional management capabilities as well as the leadership, change, and organizational capabilities usually associated with executives."

In addition to interpersonal skills, political skills are necessary for the PMO to enable timely decisions and achieve co-operation. Also required are presentation and public speaking skills to educate, tell the story, and to obtain agreement and acceptance from others.

Blanchard, et. al., (1990)[29] says that, "Managers must educate and develop the team to the point that they can take more responsibility for their work." It also says managers must give the team opportunities to perform.

The PMO displays commitment to change by supporting the team through resolution of difficult issues. Achieving project implementation success usually requires changes within an organization that should be reinforced. Developing change at an executive level and cascading it throughout the organization is an iterative process.

There are a number of goals that a PMO should strive for according to Ernst & Young, LLP (1997)[30] including:

- ❖   "Assist in solidifying the business case

- ❖   Communicate the vision

- ❖   Create a clear understanding and passion about why change is necessary

- ❖   Serve as a role model for change."

PMO behavior can be viewed as a barometer of commitment to and support of change. When a PMO and management embrace change, probability for a successful implementation increases.

PMO Responsibilities

One or more staff may occupy the Program Management Office, depending on the size or complexity of the project. It has the responsibility to:

- ❖ Conduct project initiation, planning, execution, and closure

- ❖ Define work plans, milestones, and deliverables

- ❖ Select, train, lead, and assimilate resources into a cohesive team

- ❖ Measure and report progress against work plans

- ❖ Manage project budget

- ❖ Monitor and report status

- ❖ Develop, measure, and monitor quality standards

- ❖ Facilitate issue resolution

- ❖ Develop and maintain risk management and mitigation

- ❖ Manage change control process

- ❖ Maintain project documentation

- ❖ Manage acceptance and approval of deliverables

❖   Foster communication between and among pro-
       jects, teams, stakeholders, sponsors, and man-
       agement.

PMO Skills and Abilities

Skills and abilities for a PMO range from above average personal characteristics to remaining technically as-
tute. Various skills and abilities required of a PMO should
at least, include:

❖   Ability to listen first then speak

❖   Ability to facilitate a team process

❖   Ability to communicate verbally

❖   Excellent writing skills

❖   Exemplary interpersonal skills

❖   Educated and experienced project management
       and technical skills

❖   Sound negotiating and compromising skills

❖   Skill to understand business processes

❖   Ability to focus on the big picture and details si-
       multaneously

❖   Skill to balance quality, risk, budget, dates, and
       deliverables in proper perspective to each other

❖   Ability to remain calm under extreme pressure

❖   Ability to seek and use advice from peers, man-
       agement, and teams

❖ Ability to maintain complete integrity with all stakeholders, sponsors, team members, and management

❖ Ability to make difficult decisions quickly, with minimum input

❖ Ability to plan, organize, and delegate tasks for a diverse team

❖ Ability to identify and facilitate issue resolution.

The overall role of a Project Management Office is to maintain effective and efficient project direction and progress. It accomplishes this through upper management and project teams by using a consistent methodology, monitoring work plans, mitigating risks, and adhering to project quality requirements.

A PMO can more effectively monitor progress if the work plan is broken down or divided into phases.

Implementation Project Management

Describing project roles, Mahoney, (2000)[31] states, "Responsibility, accountability, and authority are core to any management process. They are assigned and delineated by management structures for projects and operational services. They are closely related but distinct. Only when they are aligned will people and teams be able to work effectively."

Along with the responsibility, accountability, and authority comes the need for appropriate ability, training, and skills to carry out the duties of a PMO. Unfortunately, project managers and PMO generally evolve into their roles; they do not train for them.

In fact, Thomsett, (1998)[32] notes that, "The average commercial IT person has completed a 3 year university degree in computing before they are recruited into organizations. In addition, most IT people would obtain at least 3-5 days of formal technical education per year within their companies.

So, if we look at an 8 year veteran, they would typically have between 300 - 400 days of formal technical education! However, as they are moved into project management, the total of formal education in project management is 0 days! At best, they may receive a 1 to 3 day workshop on project management. No wonder our group... and others... have found that poorly-trained project managers are a major cause of project failure."

The previous results correspond with the results of the surveys conducted for this book.

The first step is to build realistic estimates into the project plan.

The appropriate choice of a leader is important to the process of coalescing a group into a team. According to Wakin, (2000)[33], "A top-down leader can paralyze a group from the first meeting by cueing its members to passively look on and listen. In contrast, a leader with a participatory style lets the team know that everyone's opinion counts."

Managing Time

Managing time means managing each project resource toward a successful conclusion of a project so each individual's use of time is productive, budget is wisely spent, and deadlines are met.

People who are performing necessary tasks sometimes do not complete them in the scheduled amount of time or by the calendar dates set forth. Kerzner, (1998)[34] says of planning and scheduling, "Unfortunately, scheduling techniques can't replace planning. And scheduling techniques are only as good as the quality of the information that goes into the plan."

Adding resources late in a project is usually counter productive. A crisis is not the time to add new resources. More often than not, additional unplanned resources added well into a project tend to consume more productivity from current team members than they contribute. This depletion of resources can be made up if there is enough time for new resources to overcome the learning curve and become self sufficient.

> *Time management must be monitored against scope and not allow for undefined elegance to drive unnecessary tasks.*

Time management and estimating should be more science than art. The first step is to build realistic estimates into the project plan. Time management must be monitored against scope and not allow for undefined elegance to drive unnecessary tasks. For instance, the drive to achieve the ultimate technological outcome could cause additional time to be added to a work plan. Building work plans with full team participation reduces this risk of technology becoming its own goal.

Work Plan

Building a project work plan is a process that should be shared by all members of the team. Management should have a chance to review and approve plans before work commences. Heller, (1998)[35] agrees and states, "Involve everybody in target setting to foster teamwork and consensus."

It is imperative for sponsors and stakeholders to have input during the work plan build process and to formally approve the project work plan before it is issued as final.

More work planning is described by Post, (2000)[36], who wrote, "Without planning and control, any project will become a runaway. Control begins with a detailed plan and performance targets that enable managers to evaluate progress and identify problems. System control is provided by standardized practices and procedures to ensure that teams are producing compatible output. User input and control ensures that the final project will actually be useful."

> *A properly used and maintained work plan reflects the health of a project.*
> *A static work plan reflects a stagnant project.*

Project work plans are difficult to build and more difficult to follow due to the inherent complexity of implementation projects. Projects are singular and each project exudes its own set of characteristics. These characteristics are defined by the mix of people, processes, technology, time, and budget.

A work plan is not complete until the post implementation review is complete. Plans must be continually updated and modified to reflect the reality of a project. Continuous use of a plan will dictate changes to it. Work plans become incorrect and detrimental through lack of use. A properly used and maintained work plan reflects the health of a project. A static work plan reflects a stagnant project.

While each implementation project is unique, projects in general possess a basic set of common traits. Good project plans are built from these common traits.

Milestones

Milestones briefly describe significant project accomplishments which act as primary checkpoints for project progress and possibly cost measurement. These are generally the items in work plans that produce highly visible results or significant deliverables.

A milestone could be an equipment delivery point, test result review, or provide a checkpoint for an approval. Every milestone should be tied to a deliverable or result. Projects lasting six to nine months may have from six to twelve milestones.

Every milestone should be tied to a deliverable or result.

Milestones can be used as an aid to budgeting as well as for monitoring progress. They describe significant targets that should be met without much deviation from estimates and should likely be included on the project's critical path.

One definition of project success listed in building projects is adaptable to milestone success during implementation projects as well. It states that,[37] "Project success is accumulated stage-by-stage during the project by meeting intermediate requirements for planning, development, design, and construction, which are collectively confirmed by acceptance of the whole project on completion and is assured by the prudent assignment of responsibility and risk, and the monitoring and control of required intermediate results throughout the project."

Managing Performance

A project work plan is the most effective tool for managing performance during a project. Performance management requires that planning in all areas of responsibility include steps in a work plan, which reflects scope of work and assignment of resources.

If we agree with the Gantthead website,[38] "The goal of every project is to drive it to a successful and appropriate conclusion. If not controlled, the iterative nature of project work can lead to a false sense of progress and ever increasing levels of unnecessary detail. Project control must be imposed not to create a bureaucratic layer, but to ensure that the project proceeds to its planned and scheduled ending."

Monitoring, measuring, and adjustments made without team input reduces chances for project success.

Actual performance and progress should be monitored against the work plan and corrective action taken as necessary. One approach to monitoring progress is to enlist the team in the process. As Willcox, (1997)[39] says, "Bring the team together and review with them in some detail the specifics of the quality, cost, and delivery problems the team is faced with. Ask each team member what he or she thinks are causing these problems. Then ask them, if there were no constraints, what would they do to fix them."

Project work plans should be dynamic and allow for revisions as projects progress. In addition, plans should allow for performance monitoring and reviews. Monitoring, measuring, and adjustments made without team input reduces chances for project success.

Another method of managing performance is to determine if the team has achieved the desired results. Capezio, (1998)[40] suggests how to measure success, "An evaluation of the team's output is conducted by an assessment of both its customers and management sponsors."

Managing Issues

An issue is any unresolved matter that may impede project progress. Issues can impair a project by impacting deliverables, timelines, budgets, or team dynamics. Impacts can be both positive and negative.

The art and science of issue management is deciding when to document something as an issue. Many questions and issues are raised during a project and some are easily answered. Others require documentation, evaluation, decision, and approval. Judgment is required to decide whether to document an issue or simply resolve and continue on.

A few basic questions can assist in determining whether the matter at hand is truly an issue. The first question to be asked should determine relevancy, if it is not relevant to the project, it is not an issue for the project.

Other questions to be asked is whether the matter at hand could delay the project, hinder quality, or increase project cost. If the answer is yes, it is likely an issue.

Even minor issues, formally presented with resolutions, should be documented to provide an audit trail. Issue logs frequently provide excellent input for Lessons Learned toward the end of a project.

Issues management includes defined roles, responsibilities, and procedures to support identifying, tracking, and resolving issues that arise during the course of a project. It provides status of issues and mechanisms to track and report issues management activities.

Effective issues management provides clear communication to team members, users, stakeholders, management, and sponsors.

The PMO should be responsible for resolving issues and maintaining an issue log. Issue resolutions that exceed the authority of the PMO should be escalated for resolution.

Managing Scope

Scope control starts on day one. Every project should have a corresponding Charter or project agreement. Even if you're just one developer trying to make the boss happy, you'll benefit greatly from documenting scope before you begin.

> *Scope control starts on day one. It must be defined before it can be managed.*

Scope must be defined before it can be managed. It should be concise, yet complete. Verzuh, (1999)[41] says, "The scope statement should describe the major activities of the project in such a way that it will be absolutely clear if extra work is added later on."

Scope definition and management are developed during charter preparation and should be closely monitored throughout the project life cycle.

Scope management can be achieved by following the "what's in" and "what's out" sections of a charter. It should quantitatively describe what is to be accomplished in order to make work planning and project budgeting easier.

Effective scope management reduces project risks and provides a solid foundation for issue and change management.

Project scope is the output of the vision and project requirements definition. It defines boundaries around the project. It specifies the original agreement between the project team and stakeholders. A properly defined and agreed to project scope reduces false expectations and assists the PMO to accurately plan.

Managing scope and change management are related but not necessarily directly linked. Some changes during a project are necessary, sought, and accommodated without a change in scope.

Scope creep has been found to be an important determining factor of project failure. Many projects end in failure due to an inability to effectively manage scope. Common causes of project failure stem from inadequately defined requirements, uncontrolled changes, and improper scope management.

Expansion of scope should be acceptable only with user and Sponsor understanding and approval. The PMO is responsible for monitoring and documenting changes to a project, such as cost, time, quality, and resources.

Sponsors initiate a project with some idea of the end result in mind. If the PMO does its job well, that idea is translated into the project scope.

Business needs can change during the course of a project and scope must be updated to reflect new requirements based on those needs.

The scope control process must be managed and controlled so that the definition of success does not change sufficiently as to guarantee project failure.

Inaccurate estimates based on ill defined scope are another major cause of less than acceptable project performance results. When initial project estimates are developed, there can be a vagueness about which form the project will take. This is true for tasks, as well as actual goals, which can change as work progresses. However, as scope is refined, estimates must be firmed, work plans adjusted, and new agreements must be sought from the Project Sponsor and project stakeholders.

> *You run a greater risk of project failure by not attempting to define scope in the first place, than by attempting the change the scope after it has been defined and agreed to.*

These elements may change the original project requirements to the point as Anthes, (1994)[42] reported, "44% of respondents said poor requirements definition is the reason for scope creep. Furthermore, only 16% of the project managers say 'No' to user requests for significant changes well into the development cycle." The numbers have not changed much since then.

The process for changing requirements or scope is natural, to be expected, and should be a part of an implementation project methodology. Only by acknowledging and managing initial scope definition can scope creep be controlled.

In spite of all of the rhetoric above, more projects fail due to a lack of initial scope definition than due to scope creep allowed after a proper definition has been accepted by the team and stakeholders.

In other words, you run a greater risk of project failure by not attempting to define scope in the first place, than by attempting the change the scope after it has been defined and agreed to.

Managing Change

It is human nature to resist change. In order to affect change, it must be perceived as having some inherent value to the person asked to change. Ram Reddy (2000) tells us,[43] "... the leader has to possess a sense of empathy and understanding of challenges facing a group before asking them to change their processes."

Once change is accepted and embraced, it must be controlled so as to maintain its usefulness toward achieving the goals of a project.

Ernst & Young LLP, (1997)[44] tells us, "Change management skills can range from basic awareness of the individual transition process to mastery of planning and implementing a major business transformation. Each skill set area may contain different levels of mastery requirements due to the Project Program's impact on the business.

Major business transformations require a high degree of mastery within each skill set area to most effectively manage the changes associated with implementation."

A formal project change process should be contained in the project charter, which also specifies the original project scope.

A change request process is used to document subsequent changes to the original project scope. As part of that process, proposed changes should be documented, investigated, and accepted or rejected.

Change Management Process

Project team members should be change agents and sensitive to the role they play in business change management. They control the nature and pace of change based on goals and objectives of a project.

Change management involves three steps; requests, reviews, and decisions.

All requests for change should include:

❖   Requestor

❖   Date of request

❖   Description of the reason for change

❖   Description of the change

❖   Justification

❖   Constraints and potential impact.

Change review should include a determination of whether the request for change might alter project scope. Other items to be considered during change reviews include a review of work plan tasks with level of effort, resources, potential costs, and duration.

Change reviews should always include a risk analysis of both cause and effect of the proposed change.

The PMO should also consider the risk of making a requested change versus not making a requested change.

The approval for change should trigger communications and documentation regarding decisions as well as changes caused by the approval.

Changes cannot be accomplished without effect on some other part of a project. These effects can be either positive or negative and can cause unrelated impacts if not monitored.

A change management process should ensure understanding of the impact each change has on the rest of a project. Probability of impact should be determined once the impact has been identified.

Some changes may be significant, but the probability of project impact can be slight, depending on resource requirements. An example might be adding a standard interface that closely resembles one previously completed. The work effort is slight, but the change provides a major positive change to process.

Benefits of change management include managing scope and reducing risks.

Managing Risk

Risk management is a process to deal with how likely a desirable or undesirable event will happen and how likely and to what extent that event could impact the project. Obviously, it is better to avoid risk altogether than to manage it.

The first step toward avoiding risk is to identify it. Lewis, (1998)[45] asks the following question. "What could go wrong that could impact the schedule, cost, performance, or scope in the project?"

Evaluating work plans for potential risks, developing strategies to address them, and assigning responsibilities will improve chances of a successful project.

The risk management process allows a PMO to mitigate risk by reducing the likelihood of an event happening or seeking alternatives to reduce the impact of an event.

Managing project risk includes analysis, assignment, and action. This means a PMO must analyze and track potential risks or opportunities, assign responsibility for mitigation, and ensure that action is taken to take advantage of positive risks or to mitigate negative risks.

Project risk analyses should include circumstances over which a PMO cannot control (external risks) and circumstances a PMO can control (internal risks). As projects progress, risk analyses and assessments should be regularly updated.

A priority can be assigned to risks based on tolerance level, potential cost of the risk, and probability of it occurring. For example, if the cost of a risk is beyond the tolerance level and it is very likely to occur, a high priority should be assigned to the risk.

Once risks have been identified, quantified, and prioritized, alternatives and mitigators should be sought. Risks can be reduced by taking actions ahead of time and can be mitigated by reducing potential consequences or by developing a contingency plan to go into affect if the defined risk occurs.

Risk lists should be monitored during a project and actions initiated according to the priority, mitigation, and contingency plans.

Managing Resources

A PMO should be able to answer the following questions for effective resource management.

❖ Who and what are the project resources?

❖ Who should provide leadership and direction?

❖ Who should ensure project quality?

❖ Who is expected to do what, why, where, when, and how?

❖ What is the defined level of quality?

If responsibility, accountability, and authority are not aligned, valuable project resources will be wasted. Mahoney, (2000)[46] says, "Problems caused by misalignment include:

❖ Confusion

❖ Waste of time, money, and opportunity

❖ Diminished productivity

❖ Internal conflicts and power struggles

❖ Inappropriate behavior

❖ Project and service failure."

If responsibility, accountability, and authority are not aligned, valuable project resources will be wasted.

A PMO can assist the project team to successfully complete its project tasks by developing understandable goals and objectives and clarifying team roles and re-sponsibilities.

Other activities a PMO should do to effectively man-age resources and ensure quality, are to establish consis-tent procedures and set appropriate performance meas-ures along with appropriate reporting and monitoring.

Managing Quality

Quality control reviews are the main vehicle for en-suring adherence to quality standards. Quality Assurance is the source for maintaining quality standards. Managing quality increases the PMO's ability to properly manage scope, change control, and reduce legal or technical ex-posure.

How quality will be assessed should be determined during project planning and preparation. Standards and procedures must be adopted or developed. Technical checks, unit and integration tests, and other reviews must be developed and promulgated to the team early in the process.

Lewis, (1998)[47] provides excellent advice when he says, "There are three principles of quality management:

❖   "Quality is everyone's business

❖   Do it right the first time, every time

❖   Communicate and cooperate."

One objective of a good quality management proc-ess should be to define quality in understandable terms of features and functions.

Quality must be applied and audited at levels appropriate for the project and the audience. Defined and proven quality methods assure that required deliverable quality is maintained.

A project work plan should include steps for quality control practices, metrics, and monitoring mechanisms.

Quality Assurance

A project quality assurance reviewer should develop the types of project reviews and walk-throughs to be conducted and these reviews should be included in the project work plan.

A deliverable should not be considered complete until it has passed a quality review. Reviews should be conducted often enough to allow sufficient time for correction.

Quality reviewers should be independent of the build team and report directly to the PMO. Quality reviews should be conducted to determine whether the system works, if it conforms to the defined standards, and if it fulfills design requirements.

Jones, (1994)[48] says, "Projects that are in a hurry often cut corners by eliminating reviews, test planning, and all but the most perfunctory testing. This is a particularly unfortunate decision. Short-cutting a day of QA activity early in the project is likely to add 3 to 10 days of unnecessary activity downstream."

The quality review process can improve team cohesion, provide a forum for learning, and assist in maintaining high standards.

Quality Standards and Reviews

A project charter should contain all quality or performance standards which must be met during a project.

Project requirements, deliverables, and quality standards described in a project charter assist teams to meet those requirements and deliverables at the appropriate quality level. A PMO should review charter quality requirements while developing standards. The quality review process itself should also be assessed during the post-implementation review.

Quality reviews should focus on finding errors and ensure that the quality process remains constructive. Deliverables should always be reviewed by a person other than the person that produced the deliverable.

The PMO should define specific quality management roles and responsibilities for individuals to ensure project quality. These responsibilities should include reviewing all intermediate and final deliverables produced.

Reviews should be performed for both technical deliverables and project deliverables and they should be conducted throughout the project life cycle.

Additionally, quality reviews should be conducted for PMO deliverables, such as project plans, schedules, and status reports, in addition to reviews of technical deliverables, such as specifications, table builds, and test results.

Scheduling quality reviews during project planning and preparation allows a PMO to build time and resources into the project work plan for conducting reviews and completing actions resulting from reviews.

Acceptance

Acceptance is part of the quality process for determining whether requirements are met and a system fulfills its intended use. Acceptance, such as software acceptance, may be conducted often during the lifecycle of a project.

Some project deliverables are so critical that errors in deliverables could result in major financial loss, injury, or even death. An iterative acceptance process can reduce these potential errors before cut-over.

Acceptance testing focuses on intermediate and final deliverables and should be defined in the project charter.

Managing Communications

The most necessary and most time consuming portion of all implementation projects and PMO activities is and should be communications. In order for a project to be efficient, effective, and to accomplish its objective, a PMO must be a skilled communicator and provide the right information to the right people at the right time.

> *The most necessary and most time consuming portion of all projects and PMO activities should be communications.*

Communications should be a high priority throughout any project. Since there are many potential delivery methods and variations, any selected method may pose unfamiliar responsibilities to team members. This can affect everyone from sponsors to users.

Sullivan, (2000)[49] says, "In studying why projects fail, the number one reason is poor communications. Lack of

understanding by the participants regarding what is expected from them by the project manager causes more
projects to sink than any other."

Special effort is necessary to ensure that those affected, understand the specific responsibilities they and
others are responsible for. Otherwise a method intended
to make project requirements more attainable may instead
cause confusion and precipitate additional problems. Elements of communication should follow the charter, be well
prepared, and easy to understand.

Beyond distribution of information and instructions
required for performance of assigned responsibilities, it is
a matter of judgment how much more to communicate to
the team. However, there can never be too much communication to stakeholders as long as the style is consistent
and appropriate. For example, daily detail reports to the
Project Sponsor would clearly be inappropriate, but
monthly summaries may be appropriate.

Judgment is necessary to determine the form of
communication, timing, amount, and to what extent verbal
communications should be confirmed in
writing.

*Effective project
communications
can deliver actual
as well as per-
ceived quality to
the implementa-
tion process.*

Success is easier to achieve with
an efficient level of communications
available to small decision-making
teams. It is important for a PMO to
monitor whether teams are communicating effectively and if not, to take
early corrective actions.

Required timing of key decisions, such as approvals
and related lead times need to be understood, making effective communications mandatory for decisions. Interrup-

tion of the agreed to communication process can delay progress and threaten project success.

Project status meetings are a communications vehicle which crosses projects to facilitate issue resolution, knowledge coordination, deliverable consistency, and quality assurance.

Kerzner, (1998)[50] believes that, "Project managers in excellent companies believe that they spend as much as 90% of their time on internal interpersonal communications with their teams."

A communications plan should identify all scheduled communications throughout a project. The entire team is responsible for adequate communication, but the PMO is ultimately accountable for ensuring an effective communication plan is created and followed.

Communications should always be conducted directly with the intended audience and all communications should be explicit.

People have built in filters based on experience and personal goals. Trying to communicate with one person through another person usually results in a filtered message, which may cause unintended results.

Communications should always be conducted directly with the intended audience and all communications should be explicit.

Implementation projects should include a communication plan which sets expectations, builds consensus, and provides feedback.

Effective project communications can deliver actual as well as perceived quality to the implementation process.

A PMO should manage expectations by communicating what project deliverables are expected and as well as expected achievements resulting from the project. Additional communications to be included in the plan are descriptions of roles and responsibilities, as well as schedule, resource, budget limitations, and quality expectations.

Communications plans that include accurate descriptions of features, functions, and benefits of a new system help build stakeholder acceptance.

Communications tools include a project charter, project work plan, memos, correspondence, status reports, team meetings, training sessions, and meeting minutes. Other communications tools include newsletters, executive briefings, presentations, "brown bag" sessions, posters, brochures, focus groups, and suggestion boxes.

Timely communications reduces potential for rumors and misunderstandings. Communication should convey only positive emotions, if any, and focus on facts.

Presentations are a form of communications that should be used to provide status, educate, share knowledge, address concerns, and answer questions. Team presentations to small groups are a great way to provide less senior team members an opportunity to hone their presentation skills.

The project charter and work plan are the most significant communication vehicles. However, the project work plan must be accurate and updated regularly to remain meaningful.

The PMO, all team members, stakeholders, and sponsors should be responsible for communications.

Project Organization Summary

A review of project management and communications responsibilities described in this Chapter includes:

❖ *Implementation Project Management* – Projects require a skilled and capable PMO using an organized methodology in order to be successful. Planning is critical to success. The project charter and project work plan are the key documents used for managing projects.

❖ *Managing Time and Performance* - An approach for developing and maintaining an integrated work plan with its associated milestones is necessary to assist project teams to fulfill their responsibilities. Assessment of results should be part of every project work plan.

❖ *Managing Scope* - A process for keeping the original requirements in mind through the use of formal change requests and reviews should be part of every implementation project methodology.

❖ *Managing Risk* – A formal risk process should be used to identify project risks it should include risk management and mitigation strategies for eliminating or minimizing negative risks.

❖ *Managing Resources -* The approach for direction and coordination of resources is important in order to minimize budget overruns and to keep the project moving in the desired direction.

❖   ***Managing Quality*** – Quality reviews provide a formal process for maintaining quality during the project and in the deliverables from the project. Reviews and audits are important tools used to meet project goals and objectives.

❖   **Managing Communications** – The most time consuming activity during implementation projects is communicating the right information, in the right way, at the right time, to all appropriate parties. Project communications should be a continuous process and it includes verbal and written communications.

Chapter Five –
The Methodology

The following methodology is not revolutionary in its construct. However, it is singular, independent, and evolutionarily and provides a distinctive approach that can replicate success.

In addition to the tenets for project success and failure, certain guiding principles have risen to the top. The following list of project truths is not in order of significance or priority.

- ❖ Successful projects have a beginning and an end.

- ❖ A project without a work plan will fail more often than not.

- ❖ A static work plan reflects a stagnant project.

- ❖ The vast majority of projects have limited resources.

- ❖ Most projects have specific time constraints.

- ❖ Projects involving package software have limited flexibility in adapting to the way business is conducted.

- ❖ Package implementation projects always involve changing behaviors in the organization.

- ❖ Projects should be broken down into manageable phases, each with specific deliverables.

❖   Project phases should be concluded with a re-view and approval of the deliverables for that phase.

❖   Design of a final deliverable is limited to the ca-pability of the application software and the skills of the team to take advantage of its functions.

❖   Regardless of product functionality or team skills, the culture of an organization can positively or negatively affect the final project outcome.

❖   Leading and managing are different skills, both are required for project success.

❖   Risk management is imperative for a successful project outcome.

❖   Actions in one area of a project will likely affect another area of the project.

❖   If an interface works once, it is not an indicator that it will work with different conditions.

❖   A stable system environment is required for valid test results.

❖   There will never be enough time or resources to test an application under all conditions.

❖   Change control is necessary to maintain project scope.

❖   Business processes should be understood by an implementation team.

❖   The more complex a project the more essential it is to have a qualified team.

- ❖ All documents produced during a project must be dated.

- ❖ In a work plan, team accountability means no accountability.

- ❖ Increases in project scope decrease chances for successful outcomes.

- ❖ Successful projects do not end on the day of cutover.

- ❖ Lessons learned from each implementation are valuable instructions and should be maintained and widely distributed.

- ❖ A formal knowledge management process is crucial for recurrent success.

With those truths as a foundation, this hybrid methodology includes a sequence of processes and tools that can substantially reduce negative outcomes of an implementation project.

Elements are combined and grouped into a logical sequence for implementation. Presentations of those items are shown in the natural sequence as they would be performed during an actual package software implementation.

However, all tasks in any project work plan are not necessarily performed completely sequentially. There are many activities which are performed multiple times and many are also performed in parallel with other tasks.

The implementation process dictates that each business situation encountered is unique. A situational analysis must surround the outlined steps which will then define practicality, sequence, and usage for each setting.

A flexible methodology, containing tasks that could be completed in detail, summary, or even eliminated, was developed so that it could be adaptable to a wide variety of audiences, businesses, software, and circumstances.

One basic premise is that, regardless of methodology, the PMO should be educated, experienced, and should possess a basic understanding of technology and the business.

Budget, time, scope, and circumstances will dictate use of subsets and may also cause an increase or decrease of project risk management oversight.

The methodology is logically structured, self documenting, and focused on but not limited to package application software.

Methodology Description

The following supports the hypothesis that package software implementation projects can evolve from the art of installation to the science of implementation.

Phases provide for specific assumptions to be documented, specific tasks to be included in a critical path, and person specific activities to be assigned. Also included are surrounding processes to monitor, measure, and adjust direction as necessary.

This methodology consists of four phases:

❖   Plan and Prepare

❖   Define and Design

❖   Evaluate and Integrate

❖   Remediate and Assimilate.

Each phase contains detail activities, processes, and tools to be utilized. Tables containing activities to be performed during each phase are included as a summary of the narrative and to establish quick references to actions along the way. Tables which describe output deliverables from each phase are also included.

Other tables are intermittently included to further summarize specific processes and to simplify an explanation of the topic.

Plan and Prepare Phase

The purpose of the Plan and Prepare Phase is to plan for project success by identifying those elements which will define and quantify project success.

The objective is to initiate activity, and to obtain approval for scope, budget, and resources. The PMO promulgates the approved scope, methodology, constraints, and approach to the stakeholders, through the use of an initial project charter and work plan.

Implementing a Project Management Office protocol leading to a successful project requires enforcement of standards. According to Billows, (1997)[51] "The organization needs to strategically conceive projects, enforce a hard edge approval process, and commit to consistent tracking and reporting."

Early preparation and planning reduces the likelihood and magnitude of future conflicts while identifying potential risks to project success and developing mitigators for them.

During this phase, the PMO establishes an overall project structure, defines the project management approach, describes responsibilities and accountabilities, and outlines the leading, managing, and monitoring processes. This also serves to reduce the potential for project failure by eliciting and propagating project assumptions early in the process and at a level so that all team members and stakeholders understand them.

The PMO must be prepared to change and adapt as circumstances dictate by including a change management process which allows for quick action.

Activities undertaken during this phase include developing standards, metrics, quality goals, and a communication plan. Additional activities during this phase include developing risk, change, and issue management plans.

Baseline documents to be used throughout the rest of the project are also initiated during this phase. A repository of most Plan and Prepare Phase activities is primarily contained in two documents, project charter, and project work plan.

Key Questions

Four basic questions to be answered during this phase, before definition, design, and development can begin are:

1.) Where are we and how did we get here?
Answers are found in the Background, Vision, and Mission sections of the Project Charter.

The purpose of the answers is to provide a foundation for the team and stakeholders and supply them with sufficient background to explain actions taken up to the current time. It also assists in explanation of how and why specific decisions were made.

2.) Where are we going and how will we get there?
Answers depend on resources and budget available and are described in the Project Scope and Project Work Plan.

The purpose is to provide a high level direction, explain resources required and available, and detail steps that need to be taken to move toward the objective.

3.) How will we know when we are done?
   The answer is found in the Project Scope and Metrics sections of the Project Charter, and in the Project Work Plan.

   The reason this answer is important is because it enables management, the team, and stakeholders share the same target and have a defined and agreed to end in mind. It is much easier to aim at a target if you can see the target.

4.) How will we know if we are successful?
   The answers can be found in the Scope, Metrics, and Critical Success Factors sections located in the Project Charter.

   Everyone wants to succeed and businesses need to receive value for investments. It is difficult to achieve success or to know if you have achieved success if it has not been defined and communicated. From a management point of view, you can manage it if you can measure it and if you can measure it, you can make it better.

> *You can manage it if you can measure it and if you can measure it, you can make it better.*

Answers to each of these questions should be contained within a project charter including sufficient detail to proceed toward the next activities and phases. The project charter is one of the major deliverables from this phase.

During the Plan and Prepare Phase, the team should expand and add detail to the charter and work plan. The final project deliverables are defined, assumptions are set, risks are identified, project work is organized, and a project scope is agreed to, during this phase.

Also, during this Phase, project organization team roles are defined and responsibility and accountability are assigned to individual team members.

In addition, resource requirements are defined, such as, how much time, level of effort, and budget will be required to complete the project.

The planning process should provide a solid foundation for the implementation and reduce the time spent during the rest of the project. As such, this process is critical and should not be skipped. According to Davis, (1998)[52] "As a rule of thumb, every hour spent on this process saves 10 hours during the life of the project."

Plan and Prepare Activities Table

The table below lists the many activities which must be conducted prior to and as part of the completion of a project charter and project work plan.

The activities listed are not necessarily in the exact sequence in which they are performed as many activities are conducted in parallel.

Plan and Prepare Activities
Describe project scope
Plan project strategy and direction
Articulate project goals and objectives
Define project oversight
Identify fiscal constraints
Identify time constraints

Plan and Prepare Activities
Establish project organization
List project assumptions
Obtain agreement to critical success factors
Describe project deliverables
Define project control procedures
Identify staff resource constraints
Assign project roles and responsibilities
Assemble project team
Define communications plan
Choose, adapt, and teach project methodology
Choose and teach project standards
Define and teach quality metrics
Choose and adapt change management plans
Choose and adapt risk management plans
Develop project risks and mitigators list
Choose environment and development standards
Define physical constraints
Develop project work plan
Prepare project charter
Obtain approvals from Sponsor and Steering Committee
Place orders for known equipment, supplies, etc. and place delivery dates, schedules, etc. in work plan
Conduct project kickoff

Many of the activities described in the preceding table are actually building blocks of the project charter and project work plan. Information gathered and developed during these activities provides input to the project charter.

Project Charter

The project charter is one of the two most important project documents, along with the project work plan. Although they serve different purposes, the charter and work plan should be developed in parallel.

A charter is a contract for success and as such, should be understood and agreed to by all parties.

It is also one of the first documents to be completed and it formalizes the agreement between management, the Project Sponsor, and the PMO. It is the document which describes the project. It also has sometimes been given the misnomer of the Project Plan (confusing it with project work plan) and is also sometimes referred to as the Project Initiation Document (PID).

The document, by any name should contain elements of project definition and information for use by project management, champions, sponsors, business management, project teams, users, and anyone else who is a part of or affected by the project. It is a cornerstone of the knowledge repository.

Its purpose is to outline the goals, detail the scope of a project, as well as describe the project management methodology. Additionally, it depicts the effort, resources, risks, and rewards of a project as well as assumptions made regarding the project.

> A charter is a contract for success and as such, should be understood and agreed to by all parties.

The charter contains a summary and detail work plan showing how long a project will take and its expected completion date along with potential risks and potential mitigators.

It includes processes for risk mitigation, issue resolution, quality assurance, and change management. In addition, it contains a directory of all stakeholders and a repository for deliverable descriptions.

The project charter should be a living document and updated as necessary throughout the project life cycle.

In summary, the project charter describes how the project began, where the project came from, where the project is going, how to get there, who the players are, and what the measurements of success are.

A comprehensive and accurate charter reduces team confusion, increases knowledge, and is the best fear-of-the-unknown risk mitigator.

The charter and work plan together describe what should be done, why it should be done, who should be doing it, how they should do it, when it should be finished, and what it should look like when it is finished.

Included in the charter are scope, goals and objectives, analysis of risks and mitigators, processes, responsibilities, benefits, and how to measure success.

One of the primary characteristics of project charters or project work plans should be an allowance for the assumptions, decisions, and facts upon which they are constructed, to change.

The project charter should formalize the contract, between all parties and it is intended to be a living document. It should also define the authority structure and accountability relationships. As such, it should serve as an active reference and dispute resolution document for the

PMO, management, teams, stakeholders, Steering Committee, and the Project Sponsor.

These two documents should represent by-laws outlining how project teams should be organized, led, governed, trained, and controlled.

Any implementation effort is likely to be a dynamic process containing conflict where every contingency, issue, and fact of information can not be readily ascertained. The documents should be amended, changed, and updated during the course of a project life cycle while preserving and ensuring the spirit and purpose for which each was created.

Changes to the charter should be noted and the revision page updated so the latest version can be distinguished from previous versions. Distribution of changed versions must be strictly adhered to and a distribution process and list should be maintained by the PMO.

Listed below are high level elements to be contained in a project charter. A table that summarizes those elements is provided at the end of the narrative descriptions.

Purpose

The statement of purpose describes the total project covered by a charter. It provides a baseline for estimating levels of effort and timelines in a project work plan.

The project charter should describe a binding project management structure and provide for governance and operating rules with management, sponsors, team members, and all stakeholders involved with a project.

Requirements

Requirements are derived from problems management is trying to solve or opportunities it wishes take advantage of.

Specific features and functions for project deliverables may be included with project requirements.

Scope

Project scope should describe the outer boundaries of where the project begins, what is included, and where it ends. Description of the scope should include applications, facilities, organizational impacts, and temporal or time.

Scope – Applications

This portion of the scope should be a narrative or list which describes the applications to be implemented as a part of the project. Use of tables is appropriate for this section.

Scope - Facilities

The facilities narrative should describe physical locations of buildings or offices which house staff or equipment affected or impacted by the project.

Scope - Organizational Impact

Organizational narrative should outline operating policies and procedures or organizational initiatives, which may be impacted or changed by the project.

Scope - Time

The time, or temporal scope should depict the timing of the implementation, phase constraints if appropriate, and the overall calendar weeks or months duration of the project. Final time will likely not be known during the first iterations of a project charter.

A graphic in lieu of narrative is appropriate for this section.

Assumptions and Constraints

This section should include a list of all known assumptions and constraints regarding the project.

It might include a statement, such as, "This project charter is based on the following assumptions and constraints, and changes to them will impact completion target dates, budget, and resource requirements outlined."

The status of assumptions and their potential impact on the associated project plan should be tracked as part of the change and risk management processes.

Examples of assumptions and constraints might be:

❖ Company will assign staff in agreement with the timeline and assignments represented in the project work plan

❖ Project team will be empowered to make real time operational, decisions related to its specific role

❖ All business decisions required will be made within five business days of request

❖   Project team, regardless of status or role, will observe all company functions and holidays.

Goals and Objectives

Project goals and objectives specifics should be described in this section, with narrative of how they fit, complement, or fulfill organization goals.

A goal is a desire that describes a future state toward which the project team will focus its efforts. The more broad goals are, the more likely that the team and the project stakeholders may interpret them differently. Project goals should be divided into specific detail objectives.

Objectives can be described as measurable steps towards an established goal. They should be as detailed, specific, and measurable as possible. Objectives provide a short-term target for defined and measurable success.

The PMO should avoid stating constraints as goals or adding constraints to goals. A constraint might describe how much to do, how to do it, or what the budget or available resources might be. For example, "To implement the new system without increasing current budget," places a constraint on the goal of the project.

> Objectives can be described as measurable steps towards an established goal.

Constraints, such as timing, costs, or resources should be described separately as constraints, not as goals. Some apparent constraints might even be considered critical success factors as the following describes.

Roles and Responsibilities

The roles, responsibilities, and accountabilities for team members should be described in this section.

An organization chart for the project is appropriate to be included in this section.

Detail responsibilities should be included by function and by person's name where appropriate. There should be no doubt for each team member, committee member, sponsor, or stakeholder what their role is and what their responsibilities are during a project.

It is appropriate to group teams together and describe team member responsibilities as a group. This is especially true for larger projects where many individual team members share the same duties and responsibilities.

Critical Success Factors

Critical success factors can be developed of a project or from a project. An example of a critical success factor of a project might be the creation of a project work plan. Another example might be fielding of a skilled project team for the project. Critical success factors should only be developed for outcomes from the project.

> *Critical success factors should be those concrete and measurable items that define successful outcomes from the project.*

My methodology does not subscribe to critical success factors of a project. The project should not be allowed to take on a life of its own. Project related factors and statements relating to the project itself should be considered as project assumptions.

Critical success factors should be those concrete and measurable items that define successful outcomes from the project. They should be identified within context of the overall project goals and objectives.

These factors should also be within the control or influence of the Sponsor, PMO, and project team.

Appropriate critical success factors describe those items that will make projects successful. These factors should describe specific anticipated business outcomes to be achieved. They should be clear, concise, and measurable.

Examples of critical success factors from a project might be:

- ❖ System to be implemented will return a ten percent decrease in system down time within 30 days after cut-over

- ❖ Staff usage of the system will be increased by fifty percent within ninety days of first productive use of the system by the entire organization

- ❖ System to be implemented will allow information access to an additional twenty percent of departmental staff at cut-over

- ❖ Purchase order transaction times will be reduced by thirty percent within 30 days after cut-over.

In order to measure achievement of some critical success factors, a baseline must be established.

Once the critical success factors have been defined, a time must be scheduled to measure current activity against which the future activity will be compared. This measurement is usually conducted early during an implementation process.

Results of measurements should be posted to the project knowledge management data repository and maintained for later comparison.

Longer projects may necessitate taking monthly or other periodic samples of statistics to establish baselines for trends and to track changes over time.

In order to have accurate statistics it is important to measure early and measure often. If you wait to begin measurements until well into the project, you will have already affected the measurements and the baseline will be adversely impacted. For instance, if you add two staff from a department to the team, then begin to measure productivity, you will have already reduced staffing and productivity will be incorrect.

Related Projects

The purpose of this section is to identify potential competition for resources, such as staff, budget, Information Systems, or Network Operations.

Use this section to describe those circumstances or resources external to the project, which must be coordinated in order to achieve the deliverables of the project at the appropriate level of quality and within the defined schedule.

An example of related projects might be a network implementation project and a new hardware rollout project with overlapping schedules.

Other dependencies should include initiatives which may impact the project or which may be impacted by the project. These might also be identified in the risk assessment. Other examples of dependencies might include sequential training initiatives, or physical site build out, or relocation.

What's in and What's out

This very simple title usually becomes important midway into a project when a request is made to change an adjunct application.

The purpose of this section is to describe exactly which application systems are included within the scope of a project and which applications are not included within project scope.

Although it may appear obvious to the casual observer, taking the time to list the applications not included will obviate many potential difficulties later during a project.

> *Taking the time to list the applications not included will obviate many potential difficulties later during a project.*

Some charters include a list of applications which may be included later depending upon narrowly defined and selected, but currently unknown circumstances.

Tables, charts, or pictures are best used to accompany the text for this section.

Risk Management

Risk management provides for the identification, assessment, impact, and mitigation of events that may <u>adversely</u> or <u>favorably</u> affect a project. A favorable risk might be the influx of staff a few months after the project has begun. It is usually good to have additional staff, but it might impact work in process or training.

During project charter development, the PMO and team should identify and assess potential impact of events that could impair or improve the successful outcome of the project.

This process can reduce the impact of risks by development of mitigators or creation of contingency plans. Responsibility for individual risks should be assigned to an individual, who would likely be most affected by the outcome of the risk.

The risk list should be continually monitored and updated. Checkpoints should be developed and inserted into the work plan to identify risks and mitigate possible project threatening results of those risks.

Risks and mitigators should be shared with the project team, Sponsor, stakeholders, and the Steering Committee.

Risk management provides a proactive means of planning for and mitigating potential impacts to a project from known risks. If an identified risk occurs, the contingency for that risk can be exercised to mitigate the risk or to reduce or eliminate a potentially negative impact.

The use of tables for this section makes it easy to follow descriptions of risks, mitigators, and assigned responsibilities.

An example of a high project risk might be a planned change in technology during the course of the project.

Issue Management

Issues are those situations, opportunities, or incidents that occur but have not been anticipated or planned for. Like risks, issues may <u>positively</u> or <u>negatively</u> impact a project.

Issue management is a process for detecting, reporting, and resolving issues which may impact the successful completion of a project. Areas where issues may be found include the physical environment, hardware, software, resources, testing, training, and procedures.

Issue management is different than risk management. An issue management process enables the project team to:

- ❖ Detect, monitor, and resolve extemporaneous issues

- ❖ Reduce negative issues to acceptable levels

- ❖ Reduce the cost of issues

- ❖ Reduce the impact of issues.

This section should show the frequency at which the PMO or others should review the issues log to ensure that it is accurate, up-to-date, and that issues are being addressed or escalated consistent with the project charter.

Issue reporting should be described here and included as part of the normal periodic project reporting process. Descriptions of issues using examples is appropriate to teach the team what an issue is, how to spot and issue, and how to report it.

This section should also describe the process for accepting and adjudicating issue requests as well as the process for logging, monitoring, controlling, and reporting status of those issues.

Issue forms should be included within the project charter appendices for issue requests and sample issue log reports should also be displayed in the project charter appendices.

Change Management

The change management process to be followed for the project should be described in this section of the project charter.

In order to determine the potential impact of changes, a number of actions should be taken in responding to each change request, such as:

❖ Analyze the extent of change required

❖ Determine business inhibitors to the change

❖ Determine whether the project can accommodate the change in terms of resources, time, and budget

❖ Determine the business impact if the change is accepted

❖   Determine the business impact if the change is delayed or denied.

This section should describe the process for accepting and adjudicating change requests. It should also include the process for logging, monitoring, controlling, and reporting status of changes.

Forms should be included within the project charter appendices for change requests. Sample log reports should also be displayed in the project charter appendices.

Change management reporting should be included as part of the normal periodic project reporting process.

Resource Requirements

This section should include a narrative and list of resources required for the project including staff, budget, and equipment.

Participants from management, business areas, vendors, and IT named to the team should have their roles defined in this section.

Estimates of the amount of time and calendar duration for personnel, budget, and equipment commitments should also be included in this section.

Budgeting is a two way process whereby personnel, time, and equipment dictate dollars required and business needs dictate dollars available. Usually, most of the budgeting process will have been completed before this stage in a project lifecycle.

At best, project personnel resources should include executive level members of the management team, such as a Steering Committee, a Project Sponsor, an experienced project manager or PMO, and an experienced project team.

Alignment of personnel resources should be developed to match roles and skills with responsibility, accountability, and authority. Misalignment of personnel resources can cause difficulties which include:

❖ Increase project time and budget

❖ Diminished team productivity

❖ Reduction of team harmony

❖ Potential resource conflicts and power struggles

❖ Inappropriate behavior.

> *Budgeting is a two way process whereby personnel, time, and equipment dictate dollars required and business needs dictate dollars available.*

Contingency plans should be developed for key roles and skills in order to maintain momentum in the event a key resource leaves or becomes unavailable to the project.

Technology

The technology section should include a description of computer hardware, network infrastructure, as well as feeder and receiver systems required to support the project and project outcomes. Graphics and tables are appropriate for this section.

Technology - Interfaces

Interfaces that describe the information and transactions that flow into and out of the proposed application system should be included in this section. Graphics or tables are appropriate for this section.

Project Protocols and Standards

Project protocols are a set of rules and procedures defining the operating principles of a project. They should be adhered to by management, team members, and all stakeholders.

Companies generally have protocols in place and reuse is appropriate. Statements should be included describing company protocols.

If there are no current procedures which apply, specific project protocols and procedures should be developed and adapted by the team.

Project Protocol Examples

Protocol examples should include many or all of the items contained in the following table. The examples listed below are brief by design and should contain more specificity and detail in an actual project charter.

Project Protocols and Standards Examples	
Item	Example
Communications	Verbal communications for changes, issues, and risks must be followed up in writing
Design and Development	Design and development activities will adhere to current company policy
Documentation	All documentation, paper and electronic, will

Project Protocols and Standards Examples	
Item	Example
	be copied to and retained in the project knowledge management data repository
Meetings	Meetings will have a formal agenda and will be produced on the forms and according to the rules included in the charter
Minutes	Minutes must be completed on forms and according to the rules included in the charter. They should be produced and distributed within one business day following the meeting
Network Architecture	Current company protocols apply
Project Tools	Project tools will be limited to version x suite of vendor XYZ applications
Quality Assurance	Formal Quality Assurance audits will be conducted at least quarterly by a non-team member, and will include written results sent to and received by the project sponsor
Status Reporting	Status reports from all team members will be completed weekly and produced on the form and according to the rules included in the charter
System Architecture	Current company protocols apply
Testing	Current company protocols apply, unless specifically noted otherwise in the charter
Training	Application training will be conducted in the form of train-the-trainer

Protocol Status Updates

This section should include specific steps for update reporting from the lowest to the highest levels.

Each member of the team should be responsible to ensure the PMO is aware of current project status and that changes are being adjudicated, risks are being monitored and mitigated, and issues are being captured, addressed, and resolved.

Team leads should be responsible to summarize status and provide input to project managers, who should be responsible to summarize status and present to the PMO, who should be responsible for reporting overall project status reporting to the Project Sponsor and other project stakeholders.

My personal desire for any team project status report at any time, any place, or any size project is a total report consisting of a maximum one page.

The more space you allow just provides more space for non-important data to enter the report. Said another way, the more people write in their status report, the less they have usually accomplished. For instance, a phone call is not an accomplishment and should not be included in a status report.

Attending a meeting (no matter how important the meeting is) is not an accomplishment. The outcomes from the meeting are important and the outcomes should be included only if accomplished during the status reporting period.

Communications

A functional communications plan should be developed and described in this section. Methods and devices to be used between and among team, vendor, stakeholders, and other parties should be described in detail.

External communications should also be planned and described in this section. A table of audiences, communications vehicle, and frequencies is appropriate to add to this section.

Testing

This section should include all types of testing to be conducted. It should also include descriptions of what is to be tested, how it is to be tested, and the validation and remediation necessary resulting from the test results. User testing, system testing, unit testing, integration testing, volume and stress testing, etc., should all be described.

In addition, person's names or functional responsibilities should be described in this section.

Documentation rules and test script development should be described in detail.

Specific detail testing documentation should be included in the test plan. The overview, descriptions, and rules should be included in this section.

Project Deliverables

Project deliverables are the visible, tangible, and definable outputs from an implementation project process. At the highest level, these should have been agreed to by the Project Sponsor prior to project initiation.

> *Project deliverables are the visible, tangible, and definable outputs from an implementation project process.*

Major milestones and related deliverables should be described in detail in this section. Samples can be included in the appendices as appropriate.

Quality Management

Quality management should be an integral part of any project. This section should include a thorough description of the process. All team members and stakeholders should be made aware of the quality management process and quality expectations.

A quality management plan should include:

- ❖   Creation of a quality policy, and assurance that management, team members, and stakeholders understand the procedures to be followed

- ❖   Adoption of practical analysis and reporting methods

- ❖   Adoption of consistent project management methodology

- ❖   Defined standards, with built in checks and balances for software, processes, testing, training, and documentation

- ❖   Independent review, testing, and reporting

- ❖   Use of automated tools where practical

- ❖   Error detection, tracing causes, and improving processes to reduce or eliminate future errors.

Most quality management activities, such as testing and technical reviews, discover defects or improvement opportunities. A project work plan should include potential rework as a discrete task after each quality management review.

Large, medium, and small projects should all begin with the same quality management process. A quality management plan should include quality planning, quality control, and quality assurance.

Process improvement initiatives should be considered for large projects to increase the quality of the deliverables and satisfaction of the customers.

Metrics provide a firm basis for measuring process improvement outcomes. They are measurements used to help estimate projects, measure performance, and reduce risks.

The PMO can only monitor, manage, and improve what is measured. Project metrics provide the basis for improvement and should be unambiguous reliable indicators for project status. Various metrics are used to assess quality, risk, test results, volumes, progress, and individual performance. Identification and capture of metrics should be considered part of the normal project reporting process.

However, if no other metrics are being captured, the following activities can be used as a foundation to collect basic information for quality process improvement.

The PMO, Sponsor, and quality reviewer should identify a set of metrics in addition to the project financial and duration statistics gathered for project management and control. These additional metrics should provide insight into project progress, documentation adequacy, and the deliverable level of quality.

Examples of Quality Management metrics might include:

❖   Customer satisfaction with project team communication

❖   Number of major errors discovered during reviews

❖   Amount and impact of re-work required

❖   Amount of time and effort spent on issues resolution.

Quality metrics should be gathered on a frequent
and regular schedule. Satisfaction surveys may be captured less often.

These metrics should be analyzed for process improvement opportunities. The deliverable review process,
for example, might include an initial review when a deliverable is 50% complete.

Time required for a draft review should likely be off-
set by a reduction of potential errors discovered during a
final deliverable review.

The quality review process should potentially reduce
the need for re-work and increase positive outcomes.

Quality Reviewer

Role and functions of a quality reviewer should be
described in this section.

A quality reviewer should not assume responsibility
for the successful completion of a project. Wherever possible, the person assigned to the tasks of quality review
should remain independent and not perform other project
functions.

The function of a reviewer should be to increase the consistency and quality of an implementation.

Quality reviewers should assist a PMO to anticipate and minimize obstacles that could reduce the efficiency, efficacy, and outcomes of a project.

Appendices

Project charter appendices should be used for those elements that need to be addressed often or are of a length which precludes putting them in the body of the document.

Items typically included in the project charter appendices include:

❖ Team name, address, e-mail, and phone list

❖ Detail project work plan

❖ Project forms

❖ Meeting agenda and minutes formats

❖ Application descriptions

❖ Complete (company and Project) organization charts.

Project Charter Elements Summary Table

The following table provides a summary of the previous charter section elements. It provides a description of the charter item and includes suggested responsibilities for creating and contributing to the content of each item listed.

Customary and usual primary responsible parties are listed first under Responsibility column.

Project Charter Elements Summary		
Item	**Description**	**Responsible**
Project Purpose	Purpose for undertaking the project. Should fulfill management expectations and provide a description of why it has approved the project.	Sponsor, PMO
Requirements	Deliverables to be provided, including summary features and functions.	Team, Vendor, PMO
Project Scope	Applications Facilities Organizational impacts Time	PMO, Sponsor, Users
Assumptions and Constraints	Principal assumptions, constraints, and other project limitations, including the project physical environment (team work space), timeframes, deadlines, funding, skill levels, resource availability, etc. (This section especially should be reviewed with and agreed to by the Sponsor prior to publication.)	PMO, Sponsor, Users
Goals And Objectives	Describes overall goals and intermediate objectives toward achieving those goals	Steering Committee, Sponsor, PMO
Roles And Responsibilities	Roles, responsibilities, and accountabilities of all team members are defined. Organization charts also work well to depict project hierarchy.	PMO, Project Managers, Team Leads, Users
Critical Success Factors	Concrete and measurable items used to define success of the project. (Establish baseline measurements as soon as possible.)	Steering Committee, Sponsor, PMO

Project Charter Elements Summary		
Item	**Description**	**Responsible**
Related Projects	Describe competition for budget, time, resources, or dollars from other projects or activities	PMO, Team, Sponsor
What's In	List all applications addressed by the project.	PMO, Sponsor, IT, Users
What's Out	List all of significant applications that will not be addressed by the project - to avoid confusion	PMO, Sponsor, IT, Users
Risk Management	Identify, assess, and develop mitigators for potential project risks.	PMO
Issue Management	Describe the process for dealing with opportunities or incidents which may positively or negatively impact the project.	PMO
Change Management	Describe the process to accept, analyze, and adjudicate change requests.	PMO, Team
Resource Requirements	Resources to complete the project are listed, including technology, interfaces, budget, staff, etc.	PMO, Team, Users
Technology	Includes hardware, software, network, and interfaces	PMO, Team, Users, IT
Project Protocols and Standards	Rules and procedures to follow. Ground rules for the project team, such as: status reports, minutes, etc. Includes tools to be used by the team. See previous table for examples.	PMO, Sponsor
Communications	Methods of communication between and among vendor, team members, stakeholders, and others should be described. Description and use of knowledge repository should be included.	PMO, Team

Project Charter Elements Summary		
Item	**Description**	**Responsible**
Testing	Describes who, what, where, when, and why of testing. Includes unit, system, and integration testing, etc. Also describes the test script process.	Team, Users, IT
Project Deliverables	Summary of major milestones from the plan should be included with a list of deliverables from each milestone.	Team, PMO
Quality Management	Describes the process, including measurements and reporting. Must be understandable and achievable by all team members. Describes how quality will be measured and the process for doing so and consequences of not achieving proscribed outcomes.	QA, PMO, Sponsor
Appendix - Team Directory	List of team, Sponsor, stakeholders, vendors. Contains all phone numbers, mailing addresses, e-mail addresses, etc., necessary to reach anyone connected to the project.	Team
Appendix - Forms	Contains forms and formats to be used during the project, such as, agendas, minutes, status reports, issue forms, and change requests. *Forms and instructions should also be made electronically available as a package to all team members.*	PMO
Appendix - Application Descriptions	Summary description of each application included in the project	Team
Appendix 0 Organization Chart	Picture of the organization for quick reference.	PMO

Project Charter Elements Summary		
Item	**Description**	**Responsible**
Appendix - Work Plan	Summary plan should be included in the Charter body and a detail work plan should be attached as an appendix. (If this section is the last appendix, the plan can be added as a separate document without regard to pagination.)	PMO

Project Work Plan

A well developed, maintained, and utilized project plan is the single most important document and tool for projects.

The PMO and team develop the project work plan by reviewing the project goals and requirements against the trio of time, budget, and quality.

A project plan consists of a set of tasks requiring resources to attain results with a specified amount of effort and within a specified time. It should be built to align those tasks and resources into an effective and efficient sequence to deliver a successful project.

The project work plan should be broken down into manageable tasks and activities with assigned responsibilities. Groups of related tasks should be summarized. Work plan reporting should be linked to individual accountability with measurable deliverables.

Work Plan Goals and Objectives

A goal is a high-level, desired direction and should be broken down into a series of objectives.

An objective is a specific step toward achieving a goal. It should be briefly stated and define what needs to be accomplished, by whom, when, and with how much effort.

Detail tasks on a work plan can be objectives or objectives further broken down. A detail set of all tasks required to meet the desired project goals and objectives constitutes the work plan.

Project work plan development enables the PMO and team members to define what they need to do; how, when, and why they will do it; and what the deliverables and outcomes will be. It also defines the level of effort required to achieve the deliverables and outcomes.

The relationship between tasks defines the dependencies of each task and creates the critical path and overall project timeline.

The PMO should lead and manage the planning process and ensure the work plan adheres to the goals, objectives, and requirements stated in the project charter.

A more detailed project budget can be developed from a well developed work plan.

Staffing to successfully complete a project can be developed from a work plan resource requirements.

Properly developed and utilized, a project plan is one of the greatest factors leading to potential project success. Conversely, lack of a utilized project work plan is one of the single most identified indicators of potential project failure.

The detail project plan should be built from a formal methodology, establish the critical path, and formalize the:

- ❖ Agreement between the Sponsor, PMO, and team

- ❖ Assignment of duties, roles, and responsibilities

- ❖ List of tasks to perform

- ❖ Level of work effort by resource

- ❖ Task dependencies

- ❖ Sequence of events

- ❖ Milestones

- ❖ Deliverables

- ❖ Timeline and calendar commitments

- ❖ Quality management interventions.

In addition, the project work plan can be used for budgeting, payroll reporting, vendor payments, and equipment delivery schedules as dictated by the individual situation.

Constructing the work plan should consist of working from the summary to the detail for the major tasks and from the detail to the summary for timing, scheduling, deliverables, and resource planning. This top-down and bottom-up approach ensures important tasks are not overlooked.

Project planning should NEVER begin with choosing the end date. The end date of a project should be determined by the amount and complexity of work, task dependencies, budget, and resource availability.

The end date of a project should be constructed as an output from the project work plan building activities. It should not be artificially arrived at and used as an input to the planning process and work plan development.

Project work plans should be built in a substantially sequential manner to maintain an overall time view of multiple activities and projects.

The end date of a project should be determined by the amount and complexity of work, task dependencies, budget, and resource availability.

Task dependencies are established by determining the relationship between work performed on a given task with the work performed on other tasks. Relationships between predecessor and successor activities and the nature of the dependency between them, along with the amount of lag or overlap that can occur between them will automatically construct the critical path and calendar timeline for the project.

Project management software by itself, is not a significant element of project success. It is merely one of the tools used by the PMO. An important point to remember regarding project management software is that it can reduce the amount of time spent on administrative tasks.

A software package, such as Microsoft Project®, is a useful tool and can provide for PMO management of single and multiple project plans with little additional administrative overhead.

When building the project work plan, some advice from the Microsoft documentation seems appropriate.

To test the accuracy of the plan, look for:[53]

❖   "Tasks for which your team has no expertise

❖   Duration and cost estimates that are aggressive

❖   Situations where you have a limited number of resources that can do particular tasks and where those resources are fully allocated, over allocated, or may become unavailable

❖   Tasks with several predecessors

❖   Tasks with long duration or a lot of resources."

One of the features of many automated project management software packages is the use of special fields, such as Text and Number Fields. These fields are extremely useful to the PMO for building views of project activities that are not otherwise naturally delineated. The fields are completely free form and can be set up by any user.

A single line item or activity on the plan can be coded so that it appears in multiple categories. This can be accomplished within a single field containing multiple codes or multiple distinct fields containing one code each. The possibilities of coding categories and uses are limited only by the imagination.

The use of groupings and categories such as, hardware, software, training, policies and procedures, etc. are completely self-discovered depending on the PMO management style and need for details.

A specific task, such as "install x hardware" can be assigned to multiple specific categories, such as a specific application category, a hardware category, a group category for specific device types, etc.

Hardware tasks may be found in various parts of the plan and can be assigned to multiple resources and teams. As such, they are hard to track without categorizing or building some other means of linking them together. By grouping and coding items this way, the PMO or reviewer can identify all line items that belong to a specific category, regardless of whether the items are adjacent, or if they are in the same phase, or assigned to the same person.

Another example of using this technique for hardware would be to explain various types of hardware activities. Network hardware may be installed and tested by one team, while user and training hardware may be assigned to a completely separate team and found much later in the project task sequence or in another phase.

In order to select all of those line items or tasks relating to hardware, the PMO or other user could select the "hardware" type categories within text fields for an isolated review or to perform a risk assessment.

If multiple applications are being implemented simultaneously, they may each have the same identical steps and deliverables and may even share the same live date and resources. This makes various code categories even more important for use as a positive differentiator.

In order to select a view of like activities to be performed for any application across projects, a similar code structure can be used, regardless of sequence.

related training, and business commitments outside of the project.

Unavailable time can be built into most work plan software packages as a personal calendar that complements the overall project calendar. The personal calendar feature for most software can be set to not allow resources to be assigned during time scheduled as unavailable time.

More considerations for calendar planning include contingency time to account for the unexpected. A good rule of thumb is to plan for the unexpected and, when in doubt, add calendar time (not work time) to the project work plan, especially at the milestone level. This will allow a minor cushion for delays that inevitably occur. Adding calendar time for the unexpected, allows for work time to remain accurate while not jeopardizing the project completion date.

> *The most important thing that can be said about project work plans is that they must be kept accurate and reflect reality.*

Allowance for time spent in meetings and administrative activities should also be included when planning for individual work time. Although meetings and administrative tasks should not be included as tasks in the actual work plan, time for them should be factored into activities.

One technique to allow for non-deliverable or non-productive tasks is to schedule for less than eight productive hours per day. This can be accomplished in the software at the project level and will allow for unproductive project time while keeping individual task work accurate.

One purpose of allowing for this extra time in the work plan, but not at the task level, is to reduce the need for constructing the work plan at the micro level.

Plans built at the micro level begin to take on a life of their own and could eventually dictate the need for a full time resource just to keep the work plan updated. Micro level project work plan development, such as for tasks that last less than four hours, should always be avoided.

A project work plan should be a tool for project management and not a task of its own.

Micro level project work plan development should always be avoided.

Meetings are a good example to describe the balance of work plan accuracy and project maintenance efficiency. Meetings take time to plan, schedule, invite participants, develop agendas, conduct, and produce minutes. If each of these activities were listed as separate tasks, it likely could take almost as much time to update the plan as it does to accomplish the individual tasks.

Conversely, if you add the time required for each meeting sub-task to one overall line item for the actual planned meeting time, you would accommodate the meeting work effort requirements with less updates but the calendar time would be inaccurate. The reason is because preparation activities are usually completed before the meeting date and minutes are usually completed after the meeting.

Project work plans can be effective tools when properly built and utilized. Extraneous activities, such as meetings, are better handled outside of actual work plan development and maintenance. They produce no discernable deliverable, require multiple resources for small periods of time, and should not affect the critical path.

Project Work Plan Construction

Project work plan activities with associated comments are listed in the following table.

Project Work Plan Construction	
Activity	**Comments**
Begin project work plan development	A complete, accurate, current, and utilized work plan is an essential ingredient for project success.
Establish a baseline after initial approval of work plan *(A baseline is a snapshot of the work plan at a given point in time)*	Establishing a baseline allows for comparison of planned vs. actual dates during review and also can be used for future project planning. The baseline function is an automated function within most project management software packages.
Each task should have an estimate of elapsed time	Based on clock time and calendar dates
Each task should have an estimate of work effort	Based on hours of work effort required to complete the task
No task* should be included if it has a work effort of less than four hours * *Exceptions may be tasks with deliverables*	If there is less work effort than four hours, there is probably more administrative work effort required to track the task than to complete it. Meetings should not be considered as tasks and, as such, should not be included in a work plan.
Each task should have a duration of less than one week	Most tasks have intermediate steps that can be listed separately. Some tasks are impractical to break down to a finer level of detail. Wherever possible, never exceed two weeks duration for any task.

Project Work Plan Construction	
Activity	**Comments**
Each task should have one owner, that is one person, responsible for the completion of the task *For individual tasks, team accountability equals no accountability.*	Other individuals may be required for actual work on a task, but one individual should be responsible.
Each task should contain a stated or implied deliverable	A deliverable can be obvious and implied, such as documentation completed and approved. The deliverable should be described if it is not obvious.
Both project and individual calendars should be used	Utilizing both calendars should reduce the likelihood of scheduling conflicts and over committed resources.
A productive work day should be defined before the plan is developed	Some amount of time less than eight hours is appropriate. Typically seven hours is used. Detail line item tasks are defined at actual time. This allows for two tasks of four hours to take more than one calendar work day, which reflects reality.
Unexpected events will occur	Build contingencies into the project work plan as calendar days, not as increases to the amount of work effort for tasks or reduced work time allotted to individuals.
Each task should have an <u>estimated</u> beginning and end date	End date should be automatically calculated from begin date and duration or level of effort.
Most tasks should have dependencies to other tasks	Build into the work plan all task predecessors and successors. This will reduce project work plan maintenance activities and allow for "what if" type planning.

Project Work Plan Construction	
Activity	**Comments**
Each task should eventually have an <u>actual</u> beginning (start) and <u>actual</u> end (finish) date	Actual task end, or finish, dates should be entered into a work plan only after completion of the task, documentation, and approval of deliverable.
Project estimated beginning and end dates should be driven by task dependencies	Dates should not be driven by a calendar but by level of effort and resources.
Project work plans should be updated regularly	Plans should be updated at least weekly, regardless of project size or length.
Project work plans should always reflect reality	Missed dates should be rescheduled and the plan updated with new dates. The baseline function should account for changes from original plan and agreed-to updates.
Project work plans should always reflect reality	Mass work plan changes, based on approved scope changes, should cause another baseline to be developed and maintained for the project, distinct from the initial project baseline.
Project work plans should always reflect reality *(Being intellectually dishonest with a project plan is an exercise in futility and the beginning of project failure)*	Agreed to changes to the work plan and subsequent baselines should be documented and maintained in a project knowledge repository. Communications should be spread far and wide of changes - to reduce chance of confusion or finger pointing later in the process.
The actual end date of a task should be determined when the final production and acceptance of the deliverable is complete	The actual end date should reflect an actual date, not the estimated date entered in the plan.

Project Work Plan Construction	
Activity	**Comments**
A task, therefore the deliverable, should not be considered complete until it is approved	Documented approval means, signed off and filed with the project documentation. Different deliverables require different levels of approval. Specific required approvals should be reflected in work plans by task.
The sum of all tasks should not be restricted to a specific end date	The beginning date, level of effort, and dependencies of tasks should create the end date of the project. A project work plan should not start with an end date. End date, by definition should not be constructed in the beginning. During a project, the end date on the plan will fluctuate. This is normal and allows the team to adjust work effort and tasks to recover time lost. By allowing the end date to float, the PMO has an idea of the reality of progress and can adjust before it is too late.
Baseline plans should be saved at the completion of each milestone * For each new baseline iteration, add a note describing reasons for changes. Save this note with the file. * A technique that has proven effective is to use a comment field and place the comment in specific cells, such as A1, A2, etc,	Baseline plans are excellent reference material for future planning purposes. Deviations allowed during phases should also be documented in the knowledge repository.
A project work plan can not be complete until the post implementation review is complete	Cutover should not constitute the end of a work plan or end of job.

Project Work Plan Construction	
Activity	**Comments**
A complete and accurate work plan should be part of project documentation	All iterations of complete and accurate work plans should be part of project documentation!

The most important thing that can be said about project work plans is that they must be kept accurate and reflect reality.

Metrics for Success

Metrics are measurements used to help estimate, measure performance, and to reduce project risks. Measurements are tools used by the PMO to manage progress, quality, and success.

Metrics can be used to monitor:

* ❖ Management (schedule, productivity, etc.)

* ❖ Quality (number of requirements, changes, defects, risks, etc.)

* ❖ Issues (number of issues open and closed, closure rates, etc.)

* ❖ Testing (test coverage, number of test cases, test results, etc.)

* ❖ Software Reliability (Defect density, failure rate, etc.).

The PMO and team should develop potential metrics that indicate whether project objectives and critical success factors are being achieved.

Metrics should be categorized and balanced to ensure they provide a complete and accurate representation of the whole project.

Project areas which can be measured and managed by objective metrics include:

❖   Cost

❖   Effort

❖   Duration

❖   Productivity

❖   Quality

❖   Reliability

❖   Satisfaction.

Risk Management

Risk management should be an integral (but not overriding) part of any project and project planning process. Emphasis should be placed on risks associated with project size (time and resources), business requirements, capabilities (resource skills), technologies (hardware, software, networks, security, etc.), and quality.

Risks are only probabilities or indicators of circumstances that might happen to affect a project. There are certain known cause and effect activities during most projects. Many negative dependency risks can be mitigated by pre-emptive action.

Once project risks and likely impacts (Low, Medium, or High) have been agreed to and a mitigation plan developed, the overall potential for project success or failure can be better assessed. Obviously, risks that have a high probability of occurring and posses a potential high impact to the project should be addressed first.

The risk assessment process should be a group effort with the project team, users, Sponsor, and PMO. A diverse audience for risk assessment is important, as different people will have different levels of knowledge and views regarding risks.

High risk factors should be reviewed between the PMO, risk manager (if one is designated) and the Project Sponsor so that potential mitigating actions can be implemented before the project starts. This helps to reduce, manage, and mitigate potential high risks. Pro-active reduction of risk before the project begins is an important facet of active risk management.

Developing a practical risk plan reduces fear and panic when, and if the risk becomes reality. Planning should include the Who, What, Where, Why, When, and How a risk will be dealt with.

> *Pro-active reduction of risk before the project begins is an important facet of active risk management.*

Risk management review points should be included at least toward the end of each milestone to ensure risks are being addressed and eliminated or mitigated. Discipline is important for risk management because few care to deal with possibilities that may or may not occur. Careful and regular assessments will increase the comfort of the team.

The following table outlines examples of risks and potential mitigators, along with responsibilities assigned. It also shows probability of the risk occurring, impact to the project if it does occur, and affects.

Owners shown in the table are listed in sequence by level of participation. The first title listed is the primary owner responsible for mitigation of the risk. Others listed share secondary responsibility for mitigation. Table lists can be effective tools for project planning.

Risk Management Examples			
Risk	**Probability / Impact affects**	**Mitigators**	**Owner**
If the team does not buy-in to the program objectives then program benefits will not be realized	Medium / High Time, Cost	Conduct a presentation to explain to and discuss the program objectives with the team	PMO
If the change management actions are not effective then the project benefits will not be realized	Medium / Medium Performance, cost	Include change management process in the Charter. Monitor change effectiveness through metric reviews	PMO, Sponsor
If there is no formal budget and no alternative source of funding can be obtained then hardware will be delayed	Low / High Time, Productivity	Identify tasks which require funding Prepare business case for each item and obtain early approval	Sponsor, PMO
Late delivery of software will cause project delay	Low / High Schedule	Communicate often with vendor and obtain commitments in writing	PMO
Frequent power fluctuations occur	High / High Schedule, Quality, Performance	Consider purchase of UPS	Sponsor, Technology Lead

Risk Management Examples			
Risk	Probability / Impact affects	Mitigators	Owner
Less software quality than anticipated will delay test completion and hamper training	Med / Med Schedule, Quality	Review test strategy and include additional intermediate test points	Team Leads, Quality Reviewer
Changing requirements will increase scope and costs	High / Med Schedule, Scope	Management and review of change control process	PMO, Team Leads

Risk Management Strategies

The following table lists a few sample risk management strategies.

Risk Management Strategies	
Risk Factor	Risk Strategy
People	
Project team is not experienced or trained and training classes are limited.	PMO should conduct training for the project team and should coach team members on an as-needed basis.
Many departmental personnel are not proficient with a PC or the PC operating system.	Company should include PC training as part of its training program for new hires.
Process	
System does not fit current processes. Changes will include integrated processing.	Training should focus on process changes. Additional user training should be planned.

Risk Management Strategies	
Risk Factor	**Risk Strategy**
Technology	
A system test environment is not yet available for the project team.	Develop specific roll out strategy for project team based on system availability

Risk Considerations

Risk management is used to reduce some of the fear, uncertainty, and doubt (FUD) in a project. Risks should be evaluated and anticipated as much as practical.

Projects should not be completely driven by risk management and consideration should be given to the formula that *Probability times Impact equals level of action required.*

Some degree of toleration for risk is healthy and cost effective. Not all risk must be eliminated in order to have a

> *Some degree of toleration for risk is healthy and cost effective.*

successful project. For instance, if the cost to mitigate the risk is greater than the risk itself, then it is better to note the risk and proceed. Documentation should clearly state that the risk was considered and the reason for the decisions.

PMOs should consider various factors when preparing a risk management strategy. Specifically one should consider those factors that are likely to affect the time, scope, resources, quality, and budget for a project.

Anticipating risk is a good way to increase the potential for project success. Risk analysis is not a one time task. It should be ongoing throughout the life cycle of the project. Factors to think about are listed below but should not be considered all encompassing.

❖ Affect of changes for the allocation of resources to the project

❖ Impact on the project from an externally imposed schedule or time delays resulting from vendor problems

❖ Competing resource requirements from partici-pating departments

❖ Availability of the necessary expertise required to undertake the project

❖ Lack of network security

❖ Size and complexity of the project

❖ Need for testing unproven technology

❖ Physical working space may not be available

❖ Number of physical locations to be implemented

❖ Availability of project funding

❖ Impact of potential liabilities from withdrawal from the project by one or more participants.

The following is a sample of a risk table to be in-cluded in a project charter.

Risk Deliverables				
Risk	**Probability**	**Impact**	**Mitigator**	**Owner**
Describe the risk in sufficient detail for the audience	High Medium Low	High Medium Low	Describe circumstance or action which will mitigate the risk	Name of person responsible and others involved

Managing Costs

Responsibilities should be assigned for continuous checking of costs in comparison to estimates, and for follow-up corrective action and re-forecasting. These practices should be an integral part of managing any project.

A procedure should be specified for the timely identification of problems and decisions leading to corrective action. The procedure should be structured to enable the monitoring of costs and commitments as well as updating of estimates and forecasts.

Project Requirements

There should be a concise vision and specification of requirements and deliverables along with defined and documented change and risk assessment processes for dealing with the inevitable changes.

The following table lists project requirements, activities, and related deliverables.

Project Requirements	
Requirement	**Deliverable**
Control program quality	Quality Assurance plan and documentation
Control program risk	
	Risks and mitigators list
Monitor program issues	Issue management plan
Monitor program change requests	Change management plan
Report project progress	Project work plan
Align organizational performance	Project status reports, deliverable reviews, metrics collection and reporting
Monitor vendor performance, activities, contracts	Vendor and contract reviews and action plans
Develop project communications strategy and plan	Project communications management plan
Coordinate program communication milestones	
Execute program communications	
Monitor and assess program communications	

Communications

Messages, such as e-mail, voice/text mail, and printed communications should be described in this section and will likely fall within the priorities listed on the following table.

Communications Priorities		
Priority	**Content**	**Response**
Informational	Data is of interest but requires no action	None required

Communications Priorities		
Priority	**Content**	**Response**
Alert	Information requires a "heads up" and may become urgent if not dealt with	Response only required by the target of the message unless a specific response is requested from others
Urgent	Message requires immediate action	Response required as soon as possible

Voice mail and text messaging should only be used to communicate quick messages of limited content, including "urgent" messages that require immediate action. Messages should include the purpose of the call and should clearly state the date and time, action required, by whom, and when needed.

A person, who leaves an "urgent" message, maintains responsibility until the person or persons contacted acknowledge receipt of the message.

Communication from company and vendor management should be routed through the PMO for review prior to general distribution. The purpose is to ensure communications and documentation reflects current and consistent information.

Written (Word, Excel, Email, etc.,) should be the medium of choice for day-to-day project communication because the history and sequence can be maintained.

Letterhead should only be used for formal status and formal notification of significant events.

Communications Plan

It is important to have efficient internal and external communication in order to have a successful implementation project. An effective communications plan should identify all scheduled and Ad Hoc communications that will occur throughout the life cycle of a project.

The entire team should maintain responsibility for accurate and effective communications.

The following bullets show the objectives of a communications plan. Communications activities serve to inform and educate stakeholders regarding:

❖ Progress

❖ Status changes

❖ Deliverable changes

❖ Metrics

❖ Causes for concern or celebration.

Communications Methods Table

The following table assumes multi-month intermediate to large project and describes the various communications methods available to the project team.

Communications Methods		
Method	**Description**	**Timing**
Project work plan (WBS)	Project management	As needed

Communications Methods		
Method	**Description**	**Timing**
Project status meetings	To track progress of the project. Includes: *Tasks* - accomplishments of each team during the past week and tasks to be completed during the following week *Issues* – a review of open issues and plans to close them *Other* - may include general update regarding management decisions or other project related matters	Weekly
Project Charter	Contains the most recent project charter and revisions. Should have pre-defined distribution list and revisions obviously noted	As updated
Issue log documentation	Any member of the team may complete an issue form when they have identified an issue. A summary of all issues should be maintained by the PMO. Issues should be discussed at a weekly status meeting.	As needed
Change request log documentation	Contains a history of change requests and status or resolutions	Weekly or less often if no changes
Standards	Contains standards and procedures for project principles and deliverable descriptions.	As needed
Risk log	Contains potential risks and mitigation strategies	As needed
Knowledge repository	Contains all information regarding the project from inception through post implementation review. Includes all paper and electronic information pertinent to the project	As needed

Communications Methods		
Method	**Description**	**Timing**
Network	The project team should have access to a network to store all project related documentation. Examples would include: the issues and log, changes and log, risks and log, status reports, minutes, work plan, test plans, system documentation, orders, receipts, correspondence, etc. It should provide for a common place to store, share, and retrieve files. It should be organized for efficient retrieval.	As needed
E-mail	Tool to be used by the project team to communicate internally and externally.	As needed
Face-to-Face meetings	This method would be used as periodic working sessions during the project among team members and with the functional users. All meetings should have minutes taken.	As needed
Steering Committee meeting	Meetings to apprise Steering Committee of progress, maintain management commitment and support, and to deal with high level unresolved matters.	At least monthly
Project newsletter	The purpose of a newsletter is to: Provide formal, printed documentation of the project status, recent business decisions and on going communication plans. Increase knowledge about, and acceptance of project within the user community. Facilitate view that the project is linked with business decisions and success. Reinforce project and communication importance. (Also, take advantage of current internal publications for articles of interest regarding the project.)	Monthly

Communications Methods		
Method	**Description**	**Timing**
Weekly status update	Form completed by each team member, leaders, and PMO. Status should be reviewed in a weekly status meeting Sent out to all management affected by the implementation project A cover letter from the PMO or Sponsor should accompany the update and issue summary.	Weekly
Training and education	These activities offer forums that can be used for updates, changes, progress, etc.	As Required
Lunches	Informal lunches might be held at various times during the project to keep users informed and involved. Appropriate times might include kickoff, major policy or direction changes, and immediately preceding education sessions, immediately preceding go-live, and during post implementation review.	As desired

Team and user communications keep the project team and leaders up to date with the status of the project and overall project management.

Plan and Prepare Deliverables

The activities from this phase are listed in the following table along with the associated deliverables.

Plan and Prepare Major Deliverables	
Activity	**Deliverable**
Planning and Preparation	Project charter developed, distributed, approved, and accepted
	Project work plan
	Project status documents
	Knowledge transfer repository
	Project organization

	Education and training conducted
	Project kickoff conducted

Plan and Prepare Risks

Risks involved with not completing the appropriate Plan and Prepare activities include:

- ❖ Lack of focus on desired end results for the project

- ❖ Goals may not meet management expectations

- ❖ Issues may not be effectively solved

- ❖ Budget may not be sufficient

- ❖ Communications may be inappropriate

- ❖ Resources may be insufficient

- ❖ Dates may not be realistic

- ❖ Deliverables may be unclear or insufficient

- ❖ Required quality levels may not be achieved

- ❖ Team may have unclear roles and responsibilities.

Plan and Prepare Quality Assurance Questions

The following questions should be asked at the end of the Plan and Prepare Phase to ensure major activities have taken place, deliverables have been acceptable, and documentation is appropriate, accurate, complete, and up to date.

Quality review questions should be widely shared with project team members early in the process so they may be aware of what is important from an overall project perspective.

❖   Does the Quality Management Plan identify how the PMO will control the project on a weekly basis?

❖   Have all support roles and their reporting structures been identified?

❖   Have resources for all support roles been named?

❖   Have all support team members' availability and experience been taken into consideration in the project work plan?

❖   Does the Issue Management Plan indicate to whom issues are sent to, where and how the issues are stored, how often reviews are held, and the adjudication process to review and deal with the issues?

❖   Does the Risk Management Plan provide potential mitigators and an action plan for the owners of each specific risk management responsibility?

❖ Has the service level agreement between the PMO and Project Sponsor been identified?

❖ Does the project work plan have appropriate project phases, steps, dependencies, resource assignments, effort estimates, and milestones identified?

❖ Does the work plan support the direction of the project as stated in the approved project charter?

❖ Has the work plan been developed based on the charter?

❖ Does the charter summarize administration and project support?

❖ Do the project definition and charter support the business requirements?

❖ Do the project and resource schedules represent a reasonable opportunity for successful completion?

❖ Are project milestones based on completion of key deliverables and are they clearly defined by target dates and deliverable descriptions?

❖ Have project milestones been reasonably based on utilization, staffing and delays?

❖ Have major project and estimating assumptions been explained in the charter?

❖ Has a contingency timing been built in by phase and is it reasonable?

❖   Have items, such as training, expenses, facility changes, technology, supplies, project support, and contingencies been budgeted?

❖   Have all projects and activities, directly or indirectly associated with the project been identified?

❖   Have all applicable assumptions concerning the related projects and activities been identified?

❖   Does the completed project work plan reflect related internal and external dependencies?

❖   Have all deliverables of the project been identified, documented, and agreed to?

❖   Are shared resources clearly defined and taken into consideration in the work plan?

❖   Have plans for managing the relationship between external projects and activities been developed and agreed to?

❖   Are quantifiable and non-quantifiable benefits and costs defined and agreed to?

❖   Are costs reasonable based upon deliverables and resource requirements?

❖   Have all cost and benefit assumptions been defined and documented?

❖   Have critical success factors been developed, documented, and agreed to?

❖   Are project benefits supported by critical success factors, timeframes, and metrics?

❖ Have all project budget categories been included in the project costs?

❖ Are other related organizational costs included in the project costs?

❖ Has the Project Sponsor's agreement to the benefits and assumption of responsibility for implementation of these benefits been documented?

❖ Is it specifically stated whether the project by itself or along with business process redesign activities will provide the stated benefits?

❖ Does the format of the status reports match what was agreed to in the Project Charter?

❖ Does the content of the status reports match what was agreed to in the Project Charter?

❖ Does the frequency of distribution for the status reports match what was agreed to in the Project Charter?

❖ Are the Status Reports concise and easy to understand?

❖ Is the current state of the project accurately represented?

❖ Have risks and issues which affect anything in the Project Charter, been identified and documented?

❖   Have variances between planned and actual metrics been identified and reasons for these variances documented and communicated?

❖   Have variances of staffing or effort hours been identified, documented, and explained?

❖   Have variances to the schedule been identified, documented, and explained?

❖   Have variances to the budget been identified, documented, and explained?

❖   Have all active deliverables and their associated work products been identified, documented, and their status indicated by reporting period?

❖   Has hardware, software, tools, etc., impacted team work performance? If so, have they been identified and documented as issues?

❖   Do the reporting metrics indicate project team actual performance against estimates, for both this phase and for the overall project?

❖   Have new estimates been calculated and documented for all reported variances?

❖   Have metrics been provided which indicate adjusted completion information for all explained variances?

❖   Do Status Reports indicate issues and status activity, as well as any risks related to the issues?

❖ Do Status Reports indicate change requests and status activity, as well as any risks related to the changes?

❖ Has Sponsor feedback been sought, provided, and documented?

❖ Has Steering Committee feedback been sought, provided, and documented?

❖ Has user feedback been sought, provided, and documented?

❖ Have items, which require outside attention been identified and documented?

❖ Are current total project costs in line with estimated spending activities for this phase and project total?

❖ Has every document (physical and electronic) been dated?

❖ Is the Knowledge repository information appropriate, accurate, current, and complete?

❖ Have all change requests resulting from information in this Quality Assurance Review been documented and distributed?

Define and Design Phase

The purpose of the Define and Design Phase is to define, design, and document requirements for the new application system. During this phase the system is constructed and validated as an integrated software package solution. The package is installed and configured in development and test environments. These environments are necessary to develop business policies and procedures, refine customizations, plan and conduct training, and create performance measures to support the new system.

The current state, desired (future) state, and the gap that exists between them is also constructed in order to design the final system.

Tables and parameters for the new application system are completed during this phase. The impact of the new application system on the organization is developed through the future state design and gap analysis. The gap analysis identifies the gaps between the current state of the organization and the desired or future state.

In addition, the impacts of and to the organization strategic plan and business goals and objectives are defined to ensure the business case for the project remains valid.

Define and Design Activities Table

The following table lists the activities, which are conducted during this phase.

Define and Design Activities
Perform Current State (As Is) Assessment

Define and Design Activities
Design and develop desired Future State (To Be)
Perform Gap Analysis
Define criteria for system usage
Receive and test preliminary equipment
Validate base application prototype or model system
Define and develop system requirements
Refine business case
Define and prioritize potential system modifications
Define and design screens, forms
Define and develop methods
Review, revise, and develop policies & procedures
Define new and revise position descriptions
Develop key performance indicators
Measure and track key performance indicators
Define and build tables and parameters
Define backup, recovery, and security processes
Perform unit tests as necessary
Define physical site preparation needs and begin remediation
Place orders for known operating supplies, training materials, etc. and place schedules and delivery dates in work plan
Define roll-out strategy
Conduct meeting with auditors
Maintain Change management
Maintain Risk management
Maintain Issue management

During the Define and Design Phase, unique requirements are identified and built into the plan, user perceptions and expectations are identified and documented, potential new system impact on the organization is defined, and the new application system is aligned with business goals and objectives.

The new system is demonstrated and potential modifications are identified, defined, and prioritized. The system is adapted to optimize integration with the desired future state.

The actual software package is loaded during this phase and the base system is demonstrated. This is sometimes referred to as "model system," "prototype system," or "conference room pilot."

New system specifications are reviewed and potential modifications are requested.

Policies and procedures are revised and new policies and procedures are defined, developed, and written.

Position descriptions are developed or current descriptions are revised as necessary to reflect the new operating environment. Position descriptions should be reviewed again for appropriateness after the new system is deployed and revised as necessary.

A roll-out strategy which supports the cut-over and implementation is developed during this phase as well.

An important consideration during the cut-over planning process is to meet with the organization's external auditors to review the documentation necessary for an audit review. Detail process and balancing documentation should be maintained as a separate deliverable package to be delivered to the audit team at the appropriate time.

Requested system modifications or changes resulting from the gap analysis are reviewed for approval based on need, cost, and impact to the project. Approved change requests are prioritized for development, assigned to appropriate resources, and tracked for progress.

Interfaces to other systems are reviewed and designed as necessary during the Define and Design Phase.

Baseline measurements for key performance indicators are created from metrics developed for the future state. Critical success factors are also reviewed during the gap analysis to ensure that they remain appropriate and achievable.

Usually during this phase, metrics for post implementation review are developed and a baseline is created. These and critical success metrics measurements should continue to be gathered throughout the rest of the implementation life cycle. Relevant measurement data is maintained in the knowledge repository.

Current State Assessment

The current state assessment, sometimes referred to as the "As-Is" model, should be performed by the team to review current business processes that may be affected, altered, or eliminated by the software to be implemented.

The current state of the organization and the affected department or area should be assessed in order to establish the baseline from which the development will begin.

This assessment involves:

❖   High-level current process model

❖   Validated requirements

❖   Description of organization, environment, and people

❖   Technical environment description

❖   Current process strengths and weaknesses

❖   Current process performance.

An outcome of the current state assessment should be a list of potential improvement opportunities.

Future State Definition

The goal of the future state definition, sometimes referred to as the "To-Be" model, is to produce a well-defined and realistic future state model. It should be developed based on data from the current state assessment and software package functionality. The desired future state describes the future vision for the organization and includes elements of people, process, and technology.

This future state vision should describe project deliverables, new business processes, new or changed job descriptions, performance measures, and desired software functionality.

Gap Analysis

The purpose of Gap Analysis is to describe the difference between the current state of the business and where the business intends to be once the new system in fully deployed. It provides opportunities to enhance business practices by aligning activities to obtain maximum benefit from the new system.

Gap analysis results should be used to determine customizations to the application package, modifications to business processes, technology changes, and the potential affect of the application system on staff.

The analysis itself tends to be iterative with both the Current State Assessment and the Future State Solution Definition. The Current State and Future State provide input to the gap analysis. Based on the findings from the analysis, they also are further refined.

The gap analysis process includes:

❖   Confirm current business processes

❖   Confirm future business requirements

❖   Confirm future technical requirements

❖   Analyze proposed architecture and processing rules

❖   Identify functional and technical gaps

❖   Develop and refine future process models.

❖   Specify system, business, staff, and physical changes required

Gap Analysis Deliverables

Deliverables from the gap analysis process are specific to this area of the Define and Design Phase.

Gap deliverables provide the foundation for the finished design of the new application system and describe changes to the current business processes and the position descriptions for the people who perform them.

Gap Analysis Key Deliverables
Conversions, interfaces, and reports defined
Baseline processes and requirements developed
Business architecture and processing defined
Policies and procedures to be affected, defined
Desired base application system functionality defined
Application, process, and personnel function gaps defined and resolved
Application system potential modifications approved and prioritized
Key performance indicators defined and baselines developed

System Configuration

After the gap analysis is complete, application design refinements are developed. One of the important elements during the implementation process is to ensure that the hardware and network environments are configured properly so that they are capable of processing the new application system effectively and efficiently.

Security and business continuity planning should also be addressed at this time for potential revisions and strengthening. Security and business continuity planning involve much more than the technical environment. They include all of the technical environment and its process and procedures for downtime and recovery as well as user processes, with checks and balances to ensure data integrity and ongoing internal and external customer service.

Configuration Management is a set of methods and tools for systematically managing the system configuration throughout the implementation.

The Canadian IT Project Managers Handbook describes it as,[54] "A configuration consists of a set of configuration items that define the system, or a part of the system. An item is any software component, release, tool, documentation, or hardware unit required for the purpose of creating or supporting customer deliverables."

Configuration Management allows the PMO to manage changes to the base application and environment, maintain related documentation, provide discipline and control, reduce confusion, and to support consistency, traceability, and integrity of the system.

Application Design

Application design is performed to ensure that the package software accommodates the business operating processes and fits with operating environment defined in during configuration.

Steps to be included during application design include:

- ❖ Design resolution for application and business process gaps

- ❖ Configure and setup software application in new operating environment

- ❖ Define and develop interface and conversion designs

- ❖ Finalize screen designs and changes

❖   Finalize reporting requirements

❖   Define and design security and controls

❖   Present users with model application design

❖   Review and revise technology requirements.

The outputs and deliverables from the application design include:

❖   Interface design

❖   Conversion design

❖   Revised business process flow impacts

❖   Revised screen requirements

❖   Revised report requirements

❖   Updated technology requirements

❖   Complete initial system setup

❖   Complete prototype

❖   User acceptance and signoff of design.

Change Management

The purpose of change management is to provide a process for the submission of changes required or desired to implement the system. It includes a description of how the change requests will be accommodated during the implementation project life cycle.

Change management processes are developed during Planning and Preparation Phase. However, most change requests occur during the Define and Design Phase.

Change requests include people, processes, and technology. The change management plan and processes extend well beyond just the system and information technology modification requests.

A change management plan should:

❖ Establish change request links to strategic business objectives and initiatives

❖ Define change leadership, management, and accommodation training

❖ Define required or desired change

❖ Specify the reason for a change request

❖ Identify desired time frame and responsible party for implementing a change

❖ Identify, define, and quantify results expected from a change

❖ Ensure required additional resources are provided to the project.

Change Review Process

The purpose of a formal change review process is to determine the potential impact a change may have on a project.

Change request reviews allow the team to analyze and document the potential positive and negative change impacts and to discuss potential alternatives.

In addition, the change review process allows the team to understand the scope and impact the solution may have before making a decision to accept the request.

Any change review process should minimally answer the following questions.

❖   Who is requesting the change to be made?

❖   What is the business purpose for the change?

❖   What exactly is to be changed?

❖   What is the likely outcome if the change is made?

❖   What is the likely outcome if the change is not made?

❖   What is the likely outcome if the change is de-layed?

❖   Does the change request affect the current pro-ject scope (positive or negative)?

❖   How important is the change to the current pro-ject outcome?

❖   Will the change affect approved project deliver-ables?

❖   What is the priority for making the change in re-lation to other priorities?

❖ What impact is the change likely to have on the project?

❖ Will the critical path, milestones, or cut-over date be affected by the change?

❖ How might the project plan change as a result of the request?

❖ What additional resources will be required if the change is accepted?

❖ Will the change affect the project budget (positively or negatively)?

❖ Who should be notified regarding the change?

❖ Who is responsible to approve the change?

Change Management Tips

Changes happen during projects. They are a natural part of the process and should be accommodated.

Since all things cannot be known at the time a project begins, the team should be open to change. Not all change requests are bad; some changes may be positive and can increase chances of project success.

Small changes accumulated equal large change impacts to projects.

Stakeholders should remain organized and review each change request with the same amount of zeal and rigor, regardless of size or apparent impact.

Small changes accumulated equal large change impacts to projects.

Cosmetic changes should be reviewed to determine potential business process impact versus pure look and feel. Many early cosmetic change requests are to make the new application look like the old one. This type should be avoided as much as politically possible.

All changes require time and resources, some positive and some negative. The following tips should assist the PMO to view all changes equally.

❖   Avoid unnecessary application changes.

❖   Ensure all changes have a positive and quantifiable business payback.

❖   Avoid the desire to make a new system look like the old system.

❖   Modify business processes to achieve efficiencies offered by new application system instead of changing the new to ape old processes.

❖   Evaluate application modification requests to ensure that they do not break vendor warranties or impact future upgrades.

❖   Enforce complete documentation when application changes are approved and especially when denied.

❖   Enforce change management review processes for all change requests.

❖   Use current and future state models to aid with education regarding change impacts.

❖ Identify conversions, data elements, interfaces, screens, process changes, reports, budget, time, and project impact for every change requested.

Define and Design Deliverables

Activities and associated deliverables for this phase are listed in the following table.

Define and Design Major Deliverables	
Activity	**Deliverable**
Current State Assessment	Current business processes reviewed and documented
Future State Description	Detail future state description including people, processes, and technology are defined.
Gap Analysis	Documented gaps between the current state and the future state
	Process Models
	Defined gap solutions
	Preliminary performance measures for new system
Site planning and preparation	Physical plant changes made for additional power, wiring, etc.
	Equipment received, inventoried, setup, tested
	Hardware, environment, and network test results documented
	Security reviewed and changes defined
Business case development	Description of costs, benefits, and risks associated with the future state description
Key performance indicators (metrics)	Key performance indicators established, agreed to, and baseline set. Baseline numbers collected for future comparison
Configuration	Hardware, network, security, and interfaces configured to accommodate new application system

Define and Design Major Deliverables	
Activity	**Deliverable**
Application system design and unit testing	Application system with changes and interfaces designed and developed
	Application enhancement detail design completed
	Base product prototype or model built
	Implementation scope description refined
	Tables and profiles build started and documented
	Unit tests performed and results recorded
	Security, controls, and system recovery defined
Data conversion	Conversion design complete
	Conversion coding started
	Reports and screens designed developed and unit tested
	Auditor review requirements documented and included in work plan
User procedure design	Revised business process flow documents
	Policies reviewed, adjusted, and procedures documented
	Job descriptions reviewed and changed
Training	Preliminary training materials laid out, audiences selected, and courses designed
	Training methodology, site selection, plan initiated
Change communications and awareness *This item is for organizational change management, not project change management.*	Organization change communication initiated by team and management, change agents recruited and coached
	Revised business process flow documents
	System demonstrated
	Help Desk procedures reviewed, revised, and training needs defined
Data Conversion	Conversion defined, sequence developed, planning started, production readiness checklist developed

Define and Design Major Deliverables	
Activity	**Deliverable**
Audit Review	Detail cut-over process and balances of old versus new metrics
	Business continuity plan reviewed

Define and Design Risks

Risks associated with not completing the tasks and completing activities during the Define and Design Phase include:

❖ Lack of cooperation from users and team

❖ Inappropriate staff assignments

❖ Divergence of system and business objectives

❖ System may not fulfill intended use

❖ Change requests could become costly or increase project scope

❖ Processing policies and procedures may not be practical

❖ Policies and procedures may not be standardized

❖ Policies and procedures may not be updated

❖ Position descriptions may not match assigned responsibilities

❖ System may be vulnerable to unauthorized use

❖ Base system may not perform as purchased

- ❖ System potential instability may not be mitigated

- ❖ Interfaces may not accommodate data requirements

- ❖ Conversion of data from previous systems may not map to new system

- ❖ User training may not be appropriate or complete

- ❖ Increased risk of hardware, software, or network failures

- ❖ Security may be easily breached causing business losses

- ❖ Insufficient equipment to accomplish task

- ❖ Organization may not be prepared to accommodate new system

- ❖ System downtime may be excessive

- ❖ Organization may not be able to successfully recover from disaster

- ❖ Site may not be ready for users or for new IT equipment.

Quality Assurance for Define and Design

The following questions should be asked at the end of the Define and Design Phase to ensure major activities have taken place, future milestone dates remain achievable, deliverables have been acceptable, and documentation is appropriate, accurate, complete, and up to date.

Quality review questions should be widely shared with project team members early in the process so they may be aware of what is important from an overall project perspective.

❖   Have all findings and recommendations from previous review been completed?

❖   Does the format of the status reports match what was agreed to in the Project Charter?

❖   Does the content of the status reports match what was agreed to in the Project Charter?

❖   Does the frequency of distribution for the status reports match what was agreed to within the Project Charter?

❖   Are the status reports concise and easy to understand?

❖   Do Status Reports indicate issues and status activity, as well as any risks related to the issues?

❖   Do Status Reports indicate change request activity, as well as any risks related to the changes?

❖   Is the current state of the project accurately and adequately represented?

❖   Have risks and issues which affect anything in the Project Charter been identified and documented?

❖   Are statistics and metrics being consistently gathered and reported?

- ❖   Have variances between planned and actual metrics been identified, along with a reason for these variances?

- ❖   Have variances of staffing or effort hours been identified and explained?

- ❖   Have variances to the schedule been identified, explained, and documented?

- ❖   Have the variances to the budget been identified, explained, and documented?

- ❖   Have all active deliverables and their associated work products been identified, documented, and their status indicated by reporting period?

- ❖   Has computer hardware, software, or tools negatively impacted team work performance? If so, have they been identified and documented as issues?

- ❖   Do the reporting metrics indicate project team actual performance against estimates, for both this phase as well as for the overall project?

- ❖   Have new estimates been calculated and documented for all reported variances?

- ❖   Have metrics been provided which indicate adjusted completion information for all explained variances?

- ❖   Has Sponsor feedback been sought, provided, and documented?

❖ Has Steering Committee feedback been sought, provided, and documented?

❖ Has user feedback been sought, provided, and documented?

❖ Have items, which require outside attention been identified and documented?

❖ Are current total project costs in line with esti- mated spending activities for this phase and pro- ject total?

❖ Does the Project Plan completely and consis- tently represent the project steps taken?

❖ Have deviations from the project work plan been approved by Sponsor, Steering Committee, or user as appropriate?

❖ Has every document (physical and electronic) been dated?

❖ Is the knowledge repository information appro- priate, accurate, current, and complete?

❖ Have all change requests resulting from informa- tion in this Quality Assurance Review been documented and distributed?

Evaluate and Integrate Phase

The purpose of the Evaluate and Integrate Phase is to ensure that application software, technical environments, and business operational processes are evaluated, tested, and ready to be integrated into the daily work of users.

Users are appropriately trained during this phase to utilize the new system while performing their daily activities. The final purpose is to cut-over the system from build and test modes into live productive use for the daily activities of conducting business.

Training is necessary to prepare users to take advantage of new system features and functions and to integrate the system into ongoing daily activities.

During this phase, data and master files are tested and validated against output from existing or manual systems. Remaining application, integration, interface, usability, volume, stress, and regression testing, etc., takes place. Policies, procedures, and position descriptions are finalized.

Business process changes are finalized and incorporated into user procedures, job descriptions, and user training. System acceptance criteria are reviewed against the requirements and defined performance metrics.

Cut-over plans are finalized, including staffing, scheduling, and duties and responsibilities for cut over team. A decision to proceed and signoff of acceptability is made for cut-over of the application to daily productive use.

Evaluate and Integrate Activities Table

The following table lists the many activities which take place during this phase.

Evaluate and Integrate Activities
Assemble test plans
Establish system test team
Conduct formal review of test preparation
Prepare and conduct system test
Prepare and conduct functionality tests
Prepare and conduct requirements tests
Prepare and conduct usability tests
Prepare and conduct interface tests
Prepare and conduct volume and stress tests
Convert data from legacy system
Prepare and test converted data
Review and test master files, rules, and tables
Prepare and conduct regression tests
Establish security policies and procedures
Establish user sign-on authority policies and procedures
Prepare system site test data
Migrate software to the system test and train environment
Conduct Integration tests
Finalize system operating policies and procedures
Finalize user operating policies and procedures
Conduct documentation and procedures testing
Prepare training materials
Prepare and conduct training competency tests

Evaluate and Integrate Activities
Conduct disaster, recovery, and business continuity testing
Conduct security testing
Resolve all open testing items
Conduct formal review and acceptance of test results
Finalize training materials
Conduct training for team, users, operations, and management
Develop detail cut-over plan
Review and approve cut-over plan
Obtain Go / No Go decision
Maintain change management
Maintain risk management
Maintain issue management
Develop one-time and ongoing Help Desk procedures
Conduct parallel processing if appropriate
Conduct operations acceptance test and obtain formal approval
Conduct user acceptance test and obtain formal approval
Integrate system into daily operations

Testing

The purpose of testing is to determine that the application works on the system it is intended for, works with other applications, works with the data it is intended for, and that it will allow the users to perform their daily activities at a level equal to or better than prior to using the new application system.

In addition to the unit tests performed during the previous phase, further tests are required to ensure that all individual pieces function together appropriately in an integrated environment.

The testing process for packaged software should be no less rigorous than testing for newly developed code. Tests should cover normal processing and security as well as volume, stress, downtime, and recovery procedures. The sequence of testing will vary by site, application tested, resources, system setup, and other criteria.

When considering testing for application software, the minimum tests to be conducted should always include the following:

❖ System, network, and hardware tests

❖ Application software tests

❖ Interface tests

❖ Security tests

❖ Backup and recovery tests

❖ User tests

❖ Data tests

❖ Master file and table tests

❖ Volume tests

❖ Stress tests

❖ Regression tests.

> *Testing for packaged software should be no less rigorous than for newly developed code.*

Systems should be subjected to successful completion of formal testing prior to cut-over. Testing should be conducted as a continuous pre-planned process and should mimic live processing as close as possible.

Software should be tested as close to cut-over and live production as practical.

Tests should be conducted with traceable procedures, have defined pass-fail criteria, and documented with test purpose, test criteria, and test results. Documentation should also include defined test cases and descriptions based on projected operations scenarios. In addition, the system should be tested to the software contract defined features, functions, and deliverables. It should also be stress tested for peak loads.

If you fail testing, you will fail production.

Other necessary testing includes interface testing, access testing, integration testing, and recovery testing.

Since testing is an iterative process, regression testing is necessary to ensure that changes from tests have not caused previously tested software to become unstable.

A quality assurance process should be designed to review the test process and ensure that it is sufficient, accurate, and that results are predictable and acceptable.

"Michael Carpenter, project manager, Phoenix based Avnet[55] says, "At least 15% of both project dollars and time should be dedicated to the testing phase."

Mark Scheinberg, Ph.D., head of PlanView systems integration group relates that[56], "Thirty percent of our budget and timeline is spent on testing."

The final word on testing is that if you cheat on testing, you will be cheated on production. If you fail testing, you will fail production.

Test Objectives

Developing objectives for an overall test plan provides a basis and starting point for testing sets of business test cases which will be required to match those objectives. Test objectives and their checkpoints in the work plan ensure that they are evident throughout a project and provide documentation that they have been met.

Adequate testing provides a means to ensure that applications will work as intended and current systems, procedures, etc. will not be adversely affected.

The following minimum objectives should be addressed in a test plan:

❖ Assure plans and tests are organized, thorough, iterative, complete, documented, and reviewed

❖ Assure there will not be negative effects to previously working applications, data, systems, security, or networks

❖ Assure there will be no degradation in performance or usability

❖ Assure that increased users and volumes can be accommodated.

In addition, keep the team informed as changes and fixes are completed.

Training, documentation, and subsequent testing may also require adjustments as the test cycle progresses.

Test Scope

The test scope definition begins after the testing objectives have been defined. A thorough review of test results conducted in earlier phases should be undertaken to ensure that results are documented and gaps are accounted for during development of scope definition. Test scope definition should include a:

- ❖ Definition of appropriate test coverage (tests, volumes, number of tests to be conducted, sequence of events, resources, etc.)

- ❖ Description of time, effort, and resources to be applied to specific areas of functionality

- ❖ Realistic schedule and sequence of events.

Test scope may vary widely from project to project, depending on a number of factors, such as:

- ❖ Analysis of results from previous testing

- ❖ Size

- ❖ Complexity of application

- ❖ Functions controlled by application

- ❖ Impact of and potential for failure

❖ The phase and type of testing involved, (unit, integration, system, user, volume, stress, acceptance, etc.)

❖ Internal and external interfaces

❖ Time and budget available.

In addition, as with any portion of any implementation process, it is important to be specific as to which elements, including systems and interfaces, are within scope and which elements are not within scope.

Once the scope of testing has been defined, an initial test schedule can be created.

Test Approach

Do not continue testing beyond the productive results of testing.

Test approach and verification activities should be conducted as soon as possible after scope has been defined. The test team should be involved in all activities to provide input to the test effort and to provide feedback regarding documentation and training materials based on test results.

The testing approach should include the following principals:

❖ Testing, as with all project activities, should follow an organized and agreed to process

❖ Each feature and function should be tested with a corresponding defined testing activity

❖ Testing should include defined system conditions and address each inconsistency

❖   Stress testing should exceed double projected volumes

❖   Test tools, techniques, results, and deliverables should be documented and maintained in the knowledge repository

❖   Each test scenario should be documented with traceable step-by-step procedures

❖   Assignments and sequence of scenarios should be described in writing then promulgated during sessions with all participants present.

❖   Each test or series of tests should include a definition of completeness and a testing procedure.

Do not continue testing beyond the productive results of testing.

Structured Walkthroughs

Structured walkthroughs are formal reviews with the testers, review team, and builders present. They allow the team to look for errors as a group. The team should use this process to determine if the system is performing as defined.

Three outcomes of structured walkthroughs are acceptance, provisional acceptance, or non acceptance. If the result shows the system to be provisionally accepted or not accepted, a list of errors and a remediation plan should be documented.

Walkthrough outcomes should always include next steps to be taken, such as remediation or continue to next steps.

Test Risk Planning

The purpose of risk planning during testing is to determine what might cause testing to fail and to mitigate the potential failure point rather than react to it after it has occurred. Maintain documentation of potential failure dependency and mitigation actions.

User Training

The purpose of user training is to enable users to perform daily job functions and optimize benefits through use of the new system. As a side note, Project team training is usually referred to as education, to distinguish the two. Those team members who are also users will likely have both types of training.

Usually a specific role of training coordinator is part of the implementation team. The person fulfilling this role should be responsible for all training development, documentation, curricula, course content, staffing, scheduling, and competency testing.

Training should be conducted to provide the knowledge and skills required to utilize the new system for day-to-day activities. Training schedules should be projected and updated as the system is developed and more information regarding chosen options becomes available.

Plans for training materials, and scheduling begin to take a parallel track to system build and testing as each progress. Training materials may have to be updated to reflect different processes or other factors changed or discovered as a result of testing.

The training schedule should be developed for conducting sessions as close to cut-over as reasonable. This will ensure the information delivered mirrors the production system as close as possible.

Thorough information gathering assures the right skills and concepts are provided by the training. The target audience to be trained is defined, their work environment is inspected, and specific tasks to be learned are documented. Data gathering is obtained through observations, interviews, testing, and reviews of new application documentation. Processes, procedures, and position descriptions are also reviewed and used as input for training materials.

Course content and format are developed from this and appropriate system information.

Training design specifications allow reviewers to look at course content and strategy before scripts, job aids, graphics, or case studies are developed. Preliminary reviews allow for revisions prior to detail course development.

Training design, specifications, and documentation should be developed in parallel with system design and testing. Specifications and documentation should include:

* An overall description of the training materials to be used

* Overall course flow

* Specific training performance objectives

* Strategy to attain each objective

* Course content to achieve each objective

❖   Summary of tools and materials to be used for each objective

❖   Testing purpose, outline, design, and anticipated results

❖   List of space and hardware available

❖   List of name, shift, email, phone of potential attendees and their supervisor / manager name and email

❖   Calendar of activities by day.

A remediation and ongoing training plan for users who failed a test or new users who arrive after initial training should be developed and included as part of the training curriculum.

Many businesses will not allow a user to receive sign-on authority if a user does not pass a test at the end of training. Time is always an enemy when it comes to training, so an early decision regarding testing and whether failed users will be allowed to use the system should be documented to avoid last minute political conflicts.

Draft versions of all instructional materials should be developed, tested, and reviewed before masters are built. The training coordinator should review, revise, test, and finalize masters before training begins.

Multiple test runs through training courses are usually conducted to ensure materials work as designed. An effective technique to test training material is to use selected staff from the target audience and conduct mock sessions while observing their performance and test scores.

Highest quality print, audio, video, screen, and other training materials will produce the best outcomes. Copies of all materials should be delivered to the appropriate locations prior to training. All training materials should also be included in the knowledge library.

Equipment that allows use of a test application system should be available to students at the work site as soon as they have finished training. This allows ongoing practice to hone new skills before cut-over. It also aids as part of system and training testing.

A train-the-trainer approach is often used when a user group is large. This approach produces effective education and fosters system acceptance and use. Additional trainer practice should also increase competency. Trainers often become power users and provide an effective addition to the support staff.

After users complete a course of training, a follow-up analysis should be conducted to measure the user's ability to perform newly acquired knowledge on the job. Results may drive revisions which should immediately be incorporated into course content.

Conversion and Cut-Over

The purpose of Conversion and Cut-Over or "Go-Live" is to facilitate an effective, efficient, and successful transition to the new application system. This should always be accomplished with a detail cut-over plan, including specific resources and a precise sequence of timed events with built in checks, balances, and backups.

Review and balancing of pre-arranged statistics or other metrics should be accomplished at this time. The cut-over process and balancing procedures with results should be well documented and maintained in the knowledge repository.

An additional set of this documentation should be maintained for delivery to auditors. External auditors should be contacted early during the implementation process and asked for documentation requirements.

The purpose of the cut-over process is to transition the application, converted data, and user procedures into productive use. This process involves not only the technical aspects of final data conversion and environment preparation, but also final user training and a confirmation of system and user readiness.

During cut-over, the implementation environment is refined, new process and organizational performance metrics are implemented, and the system and converted data are moved into production.

Immediately following cut-over, new processes should be monitored and refined. Help Desk data should be mined for determining potential system or procedure changes as well as for reviewing system efficiency and efficacy.

At the end of the transition period, procedure manuals, training materials, and other pertinent documentation should be refined and finalized.

A well planned and orchestrated implementation project will yield an anti-climactic cut-over.

Old documentation should be logged and archived as the old system is eliminated or phased out.

System Acceptance

An acceptance process provides an effective hand-off between the project team and project sponsor. This process should also include a transfer of the system control to IT Operations. Acceptance denotes the end of the Evaluate and Integrate Phase, not end of project.

There should be a formal sign-off process to document system acceptance and to transfer support activities to the Help Desk or other appropriate support group.

Acceptance and transfer to support should be widely and positively publicized. The project Sponsor should be involved and communications should be used to not only signal success, but to publicize new support and operational procedures.

As part of the system acceptance process, the project team should officially relinquish ownership and all maintenance and support duties for the system.

The PMO and team should turn over documentation including change logs, open items, remaining change requests, open issues, etc. In addition, team members should discontinue all design, development, and system changes. The project is not complete, just the previously mentioned activities.

Early planning for responsibility change from project team to operations staff forces preparation and documentation prior to system cut-over.

The transition process should:

- ❖ Provide for documentation regarding how the delivered system meets the goals, objectives, and metrics originally agreed to as part of criteria for acceptance

- ❖ Include detail processes describing when and how the system will be moved from the project team to operations and support

- ❖ Identify activities and documentation necessary to adequately prepare operations and support resources to accept responsibility and ownership for the system

- ❖ Ensure transition to the new system is controlled

- ❖ Provide documentation of remaining change requests, open items, additional training requirements, logs, unfinished documentation, etc.

- ❖ Ensure the application system is functionally integrated into daily activities

- ❖ Ensure audit requirements have been met

- ❖ Define communications and publicity

- ❖ Provide formal documented acceptance

- ❖ Begin and end with celebrations.

System acceptance and turnover does not signal the end of a project. It only signals the end of the Evaluate and Integrate phase.

Evaluate and Integrate Deliverables

The deliverables from this phase include testing, training, conversion, formal acceptance, and cut-over from a test environment into live productive use of the system. In addition, interfaces are tested and put into use. Conversion data is loaded and balanced with current live data, if any. The application system is turned on and handed off to operations for processing and support.

The following table lists major activities for the Evaluate and Integrate Phase.

Evaluate and Integrate Major Deliverables	
Activity	**Deliverable**
Integration	Interface programs
	Conversion programs
	Interface and integration tests and results
	Custom and enhanced reports
	Change communications and awareness plan
	Change communications rollout
Testing	Test objectives, approach, and plans
	Test scripts and results
	Test issue and resolution logs
	Tested technology architecture
	Application tests and results
	User tests and results
	Data tests and results
	Master file tests and results
	Regression test results
	Acceptance test approval and signoff

Evaluate and Integrate Major Deliverables	
Activity	**Deliverable**
Education and Training	Education and training specifications
	Education and training documentation
	Education and training plan, including curriculum and schedules
	Training facilities and equipment
	Student test results
	Trained trainers
	Trained users
	Trained Operations and Support staff
	Follow-up analysis of trained users
Conversion, Cut-Over, and System Acceptance	
	Conversion and cut-over migration plan
	Conversion and cut-over migration schedule
	Conversion and cut-over support schedule
	Conversion and cut-over support team roles and responsibilities
	System documentation updated and accepted
	Production readiness checklist
	Final data conversion and all master files loaded into production system
	Interfaces turned on
	Audit package of metrics, processes and documented balances of old data to new
	Help Desk cut-over plan
	Help Desk and support procedures for cut-over and ongoing support

Evaluate and Integrate Major Deliverables	
Activity	**Deliverable**
	Production schedules
	Revised Operations policies and procedures
	Formal acceptance sign-off from Project Sponsor
	Publicity plan and dissemination
	Revised business process policies, procedures, job descriptions, and flows
	Celebration plans and activities

Evaluate and Integrate Risks

The potential risks for not completing the tasks or fulfilling the activities of the Evaluate and Integrate phase include:

❖   Test results cannot be measured or validated

❖   System errors may not be detected, documented, or corrected

❖   Cut-over and live processing could be delayed

❖   Inaccurate management information could be produced from the system

❖   Users might not be capable of adequately performing daily activities

❖   Staff may be more resistant to change

❖   Staff may likely reduce short and long term productivity

❖ Unclear understanding of system impact on the organization may develop

❖ Optimum system benefits will not be likely

❖ Confidence in capabilities of new system will likely be reduced

❖ Benefits of new system will likely be diminished

❖ Vendor and consultant contractual issues may be invoked

❖ Project costs will be higher

❖ Ongoing costs of the new system will likely be higher

❖ Related projects or work may be negatively affected

❖ Legacy systems may require increased investment.

Quality Assurance for Evaluate and Integrate

The following questions should be asked at the end of the Evaluate and Integrate Phase to ensure major activities have taken place, deliverables have been acceptable, and documentation is complete, accurate, and up to date.

Quality review questions should be widely shared with project team members early in the project process so they may be aware of what is important from an overall project perspective.

❖   Have all findings and recommendations from previous reviews been completed?

❖   Does the format of the status reports match what was agreed to in the Project Charter?

❖   Does the content of the status reports match what was agreed to in the Project Charter?

❖   Does the frequency of distribution for the status reports match what was agreed to within the Project Charter?

❖   Are the status reports concise and easy to understand?

❖   Do Status Reports indicate issues and status activity, as well as any risks related to the issues?

❖   Do Status Reports indicate change request activity, as well as any risks related to the changes?

❖   Is the current state of the project accurately represented?

❖   Have risks and issues which affect anything in the Project Charter been identified and documented?

❖   Are statistics and metrics being consistently gathered and reported?

❖   Have variances between planned and actual metrics been identified, along with a reason for these variances?

❖   Have the variances of staffing or effort hours been identified and explained?

❖   Have the variances to the schedule been identi-
      fied, explained, and documented?

❖   Have the variances to the budget been identified,
      explained, and documented?

❖   Have all active deliverables and their associated
      work products been identified, documented, and
      their status indicated by reporting period?

❖   Has computer hardware, software, or tools im-
      pacted team work performance? If so, have they
      been identified and documented as issues?

❖   Do the reporting metrics indicate project team ac-
      tual performance against estimates, for both this
      phase as well as for the overall project?

❖   Have new estimates been calculated and docu-
      mented for all reported variances?

❖   Have metrics been provided which indicate ad-
      justed completion information for all explained
      variances?

❖   Has Sponsor feedback been sought, provided,
      and documented?

❖   Has Steering Committee feedback been sought,
      provided, and documented?

❖   Has user feedback been sought, provided, and
      documented?

❖   Have items, which require outside attention been
      identified and documented?

❖   Are current total project costs in line with estimated spending activities for this phase and project total?

❖   Does the Project Plan completely and consistently represent the project steps taken?

❖   Have deviations from the project work plan been
approved by Sponsor, Steering Committee, or
user as appropriate?

❖   Is the knowledge repository information appropriate, accurate, current, and complete?

❖   Is the system documentation complete?

❖   Did an acceptable rate of users pass training and
tests?

❖   Did the system go into live productive use on the
date scheduled in the work plan?

❖   Have the auditor requirements been satisfied
and is appropriate documentation maintained?

❖   Was the formal system acceptance document
signed and filed in the knowledge repository?

❖   Is the system completely monitored, controlled,
and supported by operations and support staff?

❖   Did the system adequately pass the tests or was
it fixed and re-tested for failed efforts?

❖   Was the disposition of the legacy system properly documented?

❖ Have all Change Requests resulting from the information in this Quality Assurance Review been documented and distributed?

❖ Are post cut-over metrics and measurements being collected and reviewed?

Remediate and Assimilate Phase

The Remediate and Assimilate Phase provides an opportunity for the organization through the PMO, to review the new business processes and to fine tune the application system. It offers a structured process to obtain the benefit of hindsight into the project outcomes, the affect of the new system on the organization, and lessons learned for future projects.

This phase also allows the organization to further assimilate the new application system deeper into its daily activities and to monitor, measure, and maximize the benefits initially sought when initiating the project.

During the Remediate and Assimilate Phase, the team evaluates the project process and celebrates successes.

The PMO and team should determine if the project management and processes were adequate and the deliverables were satisfactory. Individual and team effectiveness should be reviewed.

Final lessons learned should be sought and documented. Improvements to people skills and abilities, work processes, and technology should be defined, measured, and adjusted.

Key system performance indicators should be measured and analyzed to form an improved system baseline. Critical success factors, detailed in the Project Charter should be measured and evaluated. Results should be well publicized, reviewed with the project sponsor, and adjustments made as necessary.

Application systems should be fine-tuned, remediated as necessary, and become further assimilated into daily activities.

Information gathered during this phase should be compiled into a final close-out report that should be delivered to and reviewed with the Project Sponsor.

Timeline for the Remediate and Assimilate phase should be split into two periods. Following project closure, immediate measurements should be taken, team disbandment should occur, and initial system and process functions should be fine tuned and adjusted as necessary. Minor problems should be fixed only as critical for day-to-day operations.

After a pre-defined length of time, usually sixty to 90 days, the PMO should return to obtain and review key performance indicators, assess job performance, review all metrics with the project sponsor and plan adjustments and changes as necessary. Metrics and thresholds should be adjusted to allow for increased productivity.

The work plan with yet-to-be completed items and enhancements should also be reviewed at this time.

Additional and retraining should be performed as appropriate. The initial period of use allows staff to have acquired operational skills and additional skills training will enable them to make more effective use of the system and make use of advanced and functions not remembered or not previously taught.

Remediate and Assimilate Activities Table

The table below lists the activities performed during the Remediate and Assimilate Phase.

Remediate and Assimilate Activities
Review and evaluate project deliverables
Finalize and resolve remaining change management items
Finalize and review risk management items
Finalize and dispose of open issues
Complete high level work plan, for all open items and incomplete activities
Review and evaluate project performance
Review and evaluate PMO performance
Review and evaluate team and team member performance
Review all vendor contracts for performance and deliverables
Measure and report key performance indicators
Measure and report Critical Success Factors
Conduct and document lessons learned
Conduct additional and remedial education as necessary
Conduct final knowledge transfer
Remediate system as required
Assimilate system into daily operations
Complete and file final project documentation

All projects should be consciously and formally ended. The remaining project organization should be dissolved and remaining items turned over to the maintenance organization.

Reflection should always be part of consciously ending a project. The real and perceived outcomes from a project should be based on this reflection and the results of metrics and measurements. A more accurate analysis of what has been achieved will only be as good as the description of the goals described in the Project Charter. Results achieved depend on expectations set.

Documentation

The project documentation process to plan, design, develop, produce, edit, distribute, and maintain project documents used during a project should be included in the knowledge repository and reviewed for effectiveness. Documents in the knowledge repository provide an input to the quality process and facilitate an auditable and sequential view of project activities.

Project deliverables should be identified and reviewed for potential re-use. Processes to identify documentation standards for format and content as well as for review and approval should be updated. Enhancements to the process should simplify future project activities, enhance operations, ease maintenance, and reduce ongoing costs.

Reflection should always be part of consciously ending a project.

Tracking changes during a project, sequences of implementation steps, documentation of key decisions, sequential minutes of meetings, and periodic status reports all provide project traceability.

Documentation provides for enhanced management and control of a project by providing a consistent and identifiable source of knowledge which can be reviewed by all stakeholders, compared against defined and documented criteria, and understood as a view for the current state of a project.

Knowledge Repository

Rules surrounding the population and use of the knowledge management repository should be contained in the initial Project Charter. Rules for items to be included, who can extract what information, and how distribution should be handled should be defined before the knowledge repository is populated. It should contain all the project deliverables, in any format and on any medium.

There are innumerable uses for this data during the project and after project closure. It can be used as lessons learned, and to provide knowledge for future processes.

Items to be included are project technical documentation, presentation material, work documents, quality review outcomes, communications literature, testing and training materials, and project management tools. Other knowledge management documents include newly developed and documented operating policies and procedures.

The entire knowledge management repository, paper and electronic, should be copied and turned over to the Project Sponsor at the end of the post implementation review. This should be the final step in the implementation process after post implementation review.

The all-inclusive nature of the repository dictates that care and judgment must be exercised when handling sensitive information. Rules should include appropriate use and preclude unauthorized access.

Determination of contributions to the knowledge repository should be made by reviewing all project outputs, and identifying products which might not be considered deliverables but could serve as examples of quality, completeness, or approach. Products can be methods, documents, processes, procedures, deliverables, communications, photos, and more.

Include celebration items, such as flyers, certificates, pictures of gatherings, invitations, etc.

Items, such as research papers or articles, vendor documentation, and internal publications that mention the project are also candidates for inclusion.

Official project related events documentation and mailings should be included. Project deliverables, meeting minutes, status reports, interview notes, presentations, newsletters and publications, mailings, training materials, and quality assurance reports should be added to the knowledge repository.

Vendor and other third party contracts, documentation, status reports, etc., should be included.

Each iteration of the project work plan and project charter is absolutely necessary to be included in order to show how, when, and why alterations were made.

Review potential best practice examples for their completeness, quality, or uniqueness. Identify, document, and save the best examples to use for transferring this knowledge to similar situations and for future projects.

The PMO or designated librarian should consider maintaining interesting and unusual items in the repository. Pictures taken at celebration events, meetings, or training sessions are an important historical representation of the people and events that made a successful project. Maintain copies of certificates of achievement or certificates of completion for training to be used as examples in future projects. These types of additional and interesting items may spur others to use like events to boost morale or increase team participation.

No project is perfect. Bad examples are as important as good examples and should not be discarded. Describe the knowledge gained for lessons learned. Bad examples can be as powerful as good examples and should not be underestimated.

Items that may be proprietary, confidential, or not necessarily public should be reviewed with the PMO, Project Sponsor, or other stakeholders to obtain approval for copying, distribution, or future reuse.

The knowledge management repository is the natural holding place for knowledge transfer items. It should contain all relevant documents and deliverables from a project as well as additional reviewed materials. It should also be indexed and cross referenced for easy access to specific knowledge, tools, and information.

All products used as input to or output from a project may serve as tools for knowledge transfer to the organization, as well as subsequent situational and project reuse. Reusable products logically provide a basis for future coaching and training.

Coaching is a process by which an experienced team member teaches, trains, and assists a less experienced team member. The coach monitors performance and adjusts processes depending upon the level of skills and abilities of the team member being assisted. Coaching is essential for quickly building team member skills and improving the quality of work output and should be conducted throughout the life cycle of a project.

The knowledge management repository should contain products produced before, during, and at the end of a project, up to and including post implementation review and final project acceptance documents.

Examples of documents included in the knowledge management repository are listed in the following table.

Knowledge Management Repository Items (alphabetical)
All project deliverables
All statistics and measurements produced
Baseline metrics
Budget information
Celebration details, including notices, pictures, invitations, etc.
Certificates of achievement or completion
Change logs
Delivery information and bills
Event documentation
Index of contents (searchable)
Interview notes
Issue logs
Key performance indicators, baseline and subsequent
Lessons Learned
Mailings
Meeting Agendas
Meeting Minutes
Newsletters
Photographs, from events, etc.
Position descriptions, before and after
Presentations

Knowledge Management Repository Items *(alphabetical)*
Procedures, before and after
Process definitions
Project Charter, all versions
Project review report
Project standards
Project work plan, all versions
Publications
Quality assurance reports
Reference and research materials
Requirements Definitions
Risk logs
Specifications, hardware, software, etc.
Status reports, all
Templates
Testing Results, all
Testing Scenarios
Training Materials
Training test results
Vendor contracts
Vendor Documentation
Vendor status reports

The knowledge repository should be formally and continuously reviewed, as well as backed up and stored appropriately. Team members should be provided an index of documents for future use.

Knowledge Management

Knowledge management is a constant and ongoing process beginning with the initiation of a project and culminating with the end of the Remediate and Assimilate Phase. Each project should include a formal knowledge management process.

The knowledge management repository is the foundation and documentarium for all project knowledge. It should be considered the project dictionary, encyclopedia, thesaurus, and wiki combined.

Documentation is rarely valued at time of production, but becomes more so as information and knowledge are sought. Think about your birth certificate, it is rarely important, but when it is required, there is no substitute. Try to obtain a passport without a birth certificate and you will appreciate the value of appropriate documentation.

> *The knowledge management repository is the foundation and documentarium for all project knowledge.*

Benefits of knowledge management include:

❖   Faster time to value

❖   Reduced project paperwork

❖   Reduced project cost

❖   Replicable knowledge

❖   Reduced repeat mistakes

❖   Reduced re-work.

The quality assurance process should ensure that knowledge management was effective for development of team competencies.

Knowledge management provides immediate, ongoing, and post project feedback to team members. Information contained in the knowledge management repository assists PMO to:

❖ Define standards

❖ Set expectations

❖ Maintain documentation consistency

❖ Define priorities

❖ Communicate performance expectations

❖ Facilitate mentoring, coaching, and training.

> *Knowledge management should be an evolving process built into the fabric of project management.*

Knowledge management should be an evolving process built into the fabric of project management. The process itself should be documented and incorporated into the knowledge management repository.

Knowledge Transfer

Knowledge transfer describes the opportunity to transfer knowledge and experience between current and future project participants. Team members can increase business or technical knowledge by working closely with users and other more experienced personnel.

Knowledge transfer is vital to enabling smooth transitions between projects and should be a continuous process, not delayed until the end of a project.

Project Close-Out

Project close-out defines the point after go-live and cut-over and before post implementation review. It provides a focal point to formally cease project implementation activities and to document project results.

During close-out, the implementation team finalizes remaining project documentation, develops lessons learned, turns over remaining responsibilities to the organization, celebrates success with users, and formally disbands.

Operations documentation and user policies and procedures revisions are reviewed for accuracy, accepted, and officially turned over for day-to-day processing. Temporary Help Desk procedures are replaced with ongoing Help Desk support. Post project assignments of roles and responsibilities for team members should have been previously defined. Team members are officially relieved of project responsibilities and assigned to previous, redesigned, or new responsibilities.

The process for and deliverables from a post implementation review are finalized in preparation for the next and last step in the implementation process. Responsibility for conducting the review should be assigned.

The project close-out process includes a number of key activities, such as:

❖ Review and evaluate performance of PMO and project team members

- ❖ Evaluate the efficacy of the project methodology

- ❖ Evaluate the project work plan effectiveness

- ❖ Resolve or bring forward final issues, changes, and risks

- ❖ Identify best practices for future projects

- ❖ Document lessons learned for business use and future projects

- ❖ Measure and evaluate key performance indicators

- ❖ Measure and evaluate critical success factors

- ❖ Review original and revised scope, requirements, and budget against actual performance

- ❖ Define and declare a formal end to the project.

A summary of the previous information should be contained in a project review summary report. The report should highlight what worked and what did not work. It should include recommendations for reinforcement or improvement where appropriate.

A project review summary report should include such items as:

- ❖ Team purpose, structure, size, and effectiveness

- ❖ Communication management effectiveness

- ❖ Outstanding change, issue, and risk requests and dispositions

- ❖ Change management process effectiveness

- ❖ Technical and physical environment appropriateness

- ❖ Testing planning and execution effectiveness

- ❖ Training planning and execution effectiveness

- ❖ Risk management process effectiveness

- ❖ Project management effectiveness

- ❖ Issue management process effectiveness

- ❖ Development process effectiveness

- ❖ Scope changes and effects

- ❖ Final deliverables adequacy

- ❖ Incomplete enhancements and actions resolutions

- ❖ Summary project metrics, including budget, with a review of estimates vs. actual values

- ❖ Final quality assurance review.

The project review summary report allows management to participate in one more review of the process and have final questions answered before the team disbands.

The report review allows management to make decisions regarding all open and outstanding items before they are turned over for day-to-day processing. Budget or time constraint follow-up can be developed at this time.

The close-out process affords management the opportunity to understand what it purchased against what it received, and what, if anything, remains to be accomplished by operational staff. It also provides documentation for ongoing communications with other management and staff not directly involved in the process.

Changes or additions to lessons learned should be included in the knowledge management data base, along with the final report.

The purpose of project close-out is to ensure:

❖   Lessons learned results are documented

❖   Resources are officially relieved of current project responsibilities and can be reassigned

❖   Solutions have been successfully transferred to operations

❖   All project activities formally cease

❖   Operations formally assumes responsibility for operations, maintenance, and enhancements

❖   Sponsor formally accepts the agreed upon deliverables and authorizes closure.

Project Acceptance

Preliminary acceptance occurs during project close-out but final acceptance is completed during the post implementation review process.

Project acceptance is a formal process conducted to ensure both customer acceptance and satisfaction. Project acceptance criteria and process should have been defined in the project charter.

The PMO maintains responsibility for ensuring that project deliverables are complete and the acceptance criteria defined in the charter has been achieved. The Project Sponsor should be accountable for project signoff.

Project Team Performance Reviews

Project team performance reviews should be conducted during close-out. Staff performance reviews are conducted to recognize achievement, plan for improvement, and to highlight expectations for future work.

Team member reviews should be conducted by the immediate next level of management to the person being reviewed. Individual project managers and PMO staff should be reviewed by the PMO.

Project Management Review

PMO review should be conducted by the Project Sponsor with input from the Steering Committee and team members.

Project management performance should also be reviewed during close-out. A PMO performance review is conducted to recognize achievement, plan for improvement, and to highlight expectations for future work. The PMO review should be conducted by the Project Sponsor with input from the Steering Committee and team members.

An important element of the PMO review is the input from both above and below, as the PMO affects and influences team members and stakeholders at all levels while maintaining responsibility for progress and success of the whole project through its team members.

Project Plan Review

A project plan review is performed to ensure the plan has been maintained and represents the actual status of all activities. All open or incomplete items should be copied to a new, separate, and distinct next steps work plan.

The completed project plan should represent an actual status of the approved project work plan. It should be consistent with the actual status of the project including incomplete items at close-out.

Project Budget Review

Total project costs should be reviewed against budgets for total internal and external labor, as well as associated resource costs. Other categories of cost, such as training, expenses, facilities, hardware, software, and project support should also be included in the review.

Post Implementation Review

The post implementation review should be based upon the originally approved project scope, time, and, budget with subsequently approved changes. The review includes the actual project review and action plans for further training, system enhancements, and user procedure updates as necessary. This serves a number of purposes, including measuring and documenting project success by measuring how well the project met its business goals and objectives.

Timing for the review should typically be within sixty to ninety days of close-out depending on the actual size of the application systems implemented and the critical success factors developed during the Plan and Prepare Phase.

Project estimates, risks and mitigators, open changes and requests, and project metrics are all reviewed during this process. Final decisions and determinations are made, documented, and added to the knowledge management repository.

Post implementation reviews include people, process, and technology assessments.

People reviews focus on team member contribution and potential for growth.

Process reviews focus on estimates, risk management, change management, communication, and on how the project was managed. Process reviews also focus on the effectiveness of the new business processes.

Technology reviews focus on how well the system met the requirements, how well has it been accepted, and how well is it running.

The project work plan should be reviewed in detail in order to determine how effectively the project was monitored. Davis, (1998) says that,[57] "The evaluation of the success of the accomplishment of project milestones will identify what components of the project require refining."

The entire review process provides deliverables which can be used for system enhancements and for future learning and sharing.

Conducting a post implementation review provides a positive psychological end to the project. Communications of the results can deliver actual as well as perceived quality to projects.

The following factors should be considered:

❖   Attainment of objectives

❖   Effectiveness of the project plan, project organi-
    zation, and management

❖   Appropriateness and effectiveness of project
    management methodology, principles, and prac-
    tices

❖   Measurement of key performance indicators and
    comparison against baselines

❖   Measurement of critical success factors and
    comparison against baselines

❖   Process improvement opportunities

❖   Outstanding items or activities not completed at
    the time of review.

Process improvement recommendations are an integral part of the post implementation review process. They
ensure that lessons learned and ideas for improvement
are collected, evaluated, and scheduled for operational
implementation.

Post implementation review activities should also include a review of additional education and training to further enhance the basic skills learned during the project.
Users have gained additional system knowledge through
use and are ready to accept enhanced feature and function education or training.

Additional basic and advanced training should be
scheduled during this process. This often neglected step

solidifies assimilation into daily activities and immensely increases the return on investment.

The completed post implementation review report should be examined with the Sponsor and Steering Committee and filed as the final official document in the knowledge management repository.

Remediate and Assimilate Deliverables

The following table lists Remediate and Assimilate activities and associated deliverables.

Remediate and Assimilate Deliverables	
Activity	**Deliverable**
Remediate And Assimilate	Final issue log
	Final change request log
	Final risk management items
	Knowledge management repository
	Critical success factors evaluation and analysis
	Open items work plan
	Key performance indicators baseline and analysis
	Recommended improvements document
	Project status documents
	System tuning results
Project close-out	Project review summary document
	Project and methodology review results
	Project work plan review results

Remediate and Assimilate Deliverables	
Activity	**Deliverable**
	Best practices document
	Team review findings
	PMO review findings
	Vendor contract and performance review findings
	Final policies and procedures
	Final position descriptions
	System acceptance and signoff
	Quality assurance report
	Lessons learned results
	Initial project acceptance document
	Success celebration
Post implementation review	Post implementation review plan
	Residual system remediation
	Knowledge transfer summary and transfer
	Final knowledge management repository
	Additional education plan
	Process improvement suggestions
	Final project review report
	Final project acceptance document

Remediate and Assimilate Risks

The risk of not performing the steps in the Remediate and Assimilate phase include:

❖   Optimum use of system may never be achieved

❖   Implementation difficulties will likely be perpetu-
ated during future implementations

❖   Level of success or failure may not be fully
known

❖   Team may never return to other duties and
thereby will reduce productivity

❖   Application system may never be fully implemented

❖   Budget over-runs likely

❖   Benefits of new system may be only partially
achieved

❖   System may not be fully assimilated into daily activities

Quality Assurance for Remediate and Assimilate

Quality assurance for this phase should normally be
performed as soon as possible after cutover and before
the Post Implementation Review. This will facilitate an or-
derly project closure for most team members.

A copy of the Post Implementation Review report
should be sent to the Quality Assurance leader for review
and the Quality Assurance report may be amended if significant findings result from the Post Implementation Review.

The following questions should be asked at the end
of the Remediate and Assimilate Phase to ensure major
activities have taken place, deliverables have been acceptable, and documentation is accurate and up to date.

❖   Have all findings and recommendations from previous reviews been completed?

❖   Does the format of the status reports match what was agreed to in the Project Charter?

❖   Does the content of the status reports match what was agreed to in the Project Charter?

❖   Does the frequency of distribution for the status reports match what was agreed to within the Project Charter?

❖   Are the status reports concise and easy to understand?

❖   Do final Status Reports indicate issues and status activity, as well as any risks related to the issues?

❖   Do final Status Reports indicate change request activity, as well as any risks related to the changes?

❖   Has the final state of the project at cut-over been accurately represented?

❖   Have final open risks and issues which affect anything in the Project Charter been identified and documented?

❖   Have final pre-post implementation review statistics and metrics for the project been gathered, analyzed, and reported?

❖ Have variances between planned and actual metrics been identified, along with a reason for these variances?

❖ Have the variances of staffing or effort hours for the total project been identified and explained?

❖ Has the final schedule been completed and documented?

❖ Have the final variances to the budget been identified, explained, and documented?

❖ Have final post implementation review deliverables from the project that were dependent upon a related project, been identified and completed?

❖ Have final deliverables and their associated work products for the project been identified and documented?

❖ Do the reporting metrics indicate project team actual performance against estimates, for the overall project?

❖ Has Sponsor system acceptance been obtained and documented?

❖ Are current total project costs in line with estimated spending activities for the project?

❖ Does the final Project Plan completely and consistently represent the project steps taken and their final status?

❖ Has a new project work plan of remaining open items been issued?

❖   Is the knowledge repository information appropriate, accurate, current, and complete?

❖   Is the final system documentation complete?

❖   Have internal and external auditor requirements been satisfied for the project?

❖   Is the system still completely monitored, controlled, and supported by operations and support staff?

❖   Has the legacy system been deactivated?

❖   Have all project quantifiable and non-quantifiable benefits and costs been clearly defined and documented in the acceptance document?

❖   Have actual financial and other benefits for the project been documented and supported by critical success factors, timeframes, and measurements?

❖   Are all project budget categories included in the final costs?

❖   Has the Sponsor's agreement to the final report of benefits been documented?

❖   Is it specifically stated that the project by itself, or along with other projects, achieved the benefits described?

❖   Has a post implementation review plan been developed, scheduled, and accepted?

❖ Have all Change Requests resulting from the information in this Quality Assurance Review been documented?

Summary of Major Project Activities and Deliverables

The following table lists major project activities with associated deliverables. The list is in summary form and is not intended to be complete.

Summary of Major Project Activities and Deliverables	
Activity	**Deliverables**
Project planning	Project charter including scope and project organization, project team requirements, operating and review processes, project work plan, critical success factors, and design and testing strategies
Site readiness	Site plan including all physical areas affected, includes electronic and electric wiring diagrams, physical plant modification definitions and diagrams, device roll-out plan
Technology environment	Technology infrastructure installed and configured, including servers and networks, hardware, software, and initial IT process and procedures
Environment set-up and package installation	Base package operating environment, infrastructure requirements developed and Infrastructure is built. Package installed and tested
Control vendor and contract performance	Vendor and contract open issues and action plans Signed contracts with revisions, if any Reports from monitoring vendor performance, activities, and contracts
Current and future state definition	Current and future process models Base package built for walkthrough Current and future integration models Organization performance metrics Gap identification

Summary of Major Project Activities and Deliverables	
Activity	**Deliverables**
Business case development	Final business case
	Cost/benefit analysis
	Risk assessment
Manage program communication	Program communication management strategy and plan
	Status, monitor, and assess project communication reports
Align change leadership	Program change leadership framework, requirements, and plan
	Monitor program change leadership reports
Develop stakeholder Involvement Strategy	Stakeholder involvement strategy and plan
	Monitor stakeholder involvement status reports

Summary of Major Project Documents

The following table provides a quick reference of major project documents, regardless of phase. It includes purpose or intended use of each. The list is not intended to be complete.

Summary of Major Project Documents	
Document	**Purpose**
Work plan	Defines the specific work tasks, including level of effort, duration estimates, task dependencies, and resources.
Project charter	Defines the project scope, roles and responsibilities, and the approach for managing issues, changes, risks, and quality for the project. Provides structure for ongoing project management.
Budget and cost worksheet	Shows the calculations and total dollar amounts utilized to derive cost estimates for the project.

Summary of Major Project Documents	
Document	**Purpose**
Communications plan	Details the structure for communication between and among PMO, team, and all stakeholders. Used to establish thorough lines of communication which will reduce the amount of time necessary to relay information, progress, and results.
Change request log and forms	Provides formal documentation and tracking of change requests. Contains a history of issues and resolutions. Used to track the status of issues from the time they are identified and submitted, until they are resolved or rejected. Specific process for monitoring changes is should be contained in the Project Charter.
Issue log and form	Provides for tracking and status of issues. Contains a history of issues and resolutions. Used to track the status of issues from the time they are identified until resolved or rejected. Specific process for monitoring changes should be contained in the Project Charter
Project assessment documents	Reports project review results, process improvement suggestions, and assessments of people and project performance. Includes reviews and approvals as well as client satisfaction results.
Project status reports	All status reports and actual performance data prepared for or by the PMO. Includes project status reports, performance data, post implementation review plan, and report.
Vendor and contract management review documents	Includes all vendor, package, and contract information to manage and control the quality, effectiveness, and efficiency of the vendor, support, and system.
Project performance management	Establishes project performance measures, reporting criteria, collection of performance management data, communicates performance measures, and shows issues related to project and team performance. Includes Performance measures, Reporting criteria and reports, Performance measurement Communications strategy, and Post implementation plan and review

Summary of Major Project Documents	
Document	**Purpose**
Communication log	Contains a contact directory, notices, and other correspondence for the project. Provides a record of all formal project communications and is contained in the project knowledge repository.
Protocols and standards documents	Standards for format and content of deliverables and processes. Ensures team members and stakeholders have access to, have been educated, and use the same operating principles.
Other self evident documentation	Risk log, Training plan and documentation, Cutover plan, Operations policies and procedures, Backup, recovery, business continuity documentation,
Knowledge management repository	Contains definition of how knowledge repository itself will be developed, maintained, and accessed. Includes all documents and other appropriate data, forms, correspondence, deliverables, and outputs from reviews. Serves as both input and output for project documentation. Serves as input to knowledge transfer for team and organization.

Lessons Learned Topics and Questions

Develop and distribute specific questions regarding the project and give team members time to prepare their own lessons learned individually. Seek both positive and negative lessons learned.

The purpose of thought provoking questions is to stimulate ideas that may have been forgotten. The process permits team members to develop their responses and thoughts to the questions without fear of group or management intimidation. In addition, it allows time to create more thoughtful and richer responses.

There should be no restrictions as to which questions should be answered or how they should be answered. Other comments should be actively sought with guarantees of anonymity and no risk of reprisal.

Teams should be cautioned that uses of individual names or particular personalities which can be traced to specific individuals are not appropriate or beneficial to the process. Answers should be delivered anonymously to a single member for summarization and subsequent presentation at an open meeting of team members only.

An effective technique to keep answers succinct is to request that no list should be longer than one page of bullets. This forces the teams to focus on the larger picture.

After summarizing the lists and eliminating duplicate comments, conduct a meeting to discuss customer team responses to the questions and other positive and negative comments generated from the list.

If a vendor or consulting firm is used to assist or run an implementation, consider holding separate meetings with vendor or consulting employees only and additional but separate meetings with the combined teams.

The purpose of separate meetings is to reduce the potential for stifled comments between outside firms and internal customers not wishing to share shortcomings across groups.

All responses should be entered into and maintained in the appropriate area of the knowledge management repository for future learning. They should be used to provide input for adjustments and updates to policies, procedures, methodologies, future projects, etc.

Final lessons learned should be widely disseminated in order to achieve maximum benefit.

The following sample list can be used to stimulate discussion topics. It should not be used as a strict question and answer process which leaves no room for individuality.

Sample Lessons Learned Questions
Are you proud of the project deliverables - If yes, what's good about them? If no, what's wrong with them?
What were the two most frustrating parts of this project?
If you were in charge, how would you do things differently next time?
Which of methods or processes worked particularly well and why?
Which methods or processes did not work so well and why?
If you could change two things about this project that would have provided the greatest impact for project success, what would they be?
Did the final project deliverables differ significantly from the project charter described project deliverables? If yes, what do you think were the most significant causes?
Were all team roles and responsibilities clearly defined and communicated up front? If not, what do you think could be done differently next time?
Did user training provide the required level of skills to perform new duties?
Which two parts of the testing process contributed most to the success of the project?
Did testing uncover and fix things that might have caused later failure? If so, please share two.
Describe the three most important characteristics of the person or persons who contributed most to the success of the project. (Do not include names)
List your top three negative lessons learned from this project.
List your top three positive lessons learned from this project.

Sample Lessons Learned Questions
List any other personal or professional lessons learned that you would like to share with others.
What were the two most gratifying parts of the project for you?

Lessons Learned

The previous table lists questions for use in soliciting input and should provide grist for responses.

The process advocated in this methodology seeks interaction and provides feedback from and to the whole project team. It provides maximum exposure for input as well as dissemination of output information.

Planning and drawing from lessons learned are critical to successful future implementations. Planning alone is not the sole answer to project implementation success.

New lessons learned will be uncovered during each implementation. Lessons learned from each new project will be different from previous projects and should provide a growing experience rather than a reminder of past deficiencies. Each iteration should provide rich resources and unique insights toward increasing chances of success for future implementation projects.

Final Thoughts

There are some important critical success factors related to each implementation, regardless of situational differences. Although the project management process for implementing package software continues to be dynamic, many of the roles and responsibilities, activities and deliverables of this process are not unique to package software implementations. They follow sound project management principles, such as:

- ❖ Prepare for the future by learning from the past

- ❖ Bad experiences can be as valuable or more valuable than good experiences

- ❖ A structured process provides a much better chance of success than a non-structured process.

It remains the responsibility of each practitioner to abandon those things which lead to project failure and to follow those strategies which lead to project success.

The bottom line is this. If you truly wish to be successful in life or on a project, listen to your Leader, follow the rules, live within your means, play nice together, learn from those who came before you, and celebrate success as you go.

APPENDICES

Appendix A –
Index of Tables and Figures

Appendix B - Definitions

Accountability - Owning, explaining, and experiencing the outcome of a task.

Application and Application Software – The actual program or group of programs which make up the total system to be implemented.

Authority - The power to control, enable, or prohibit a task.

Champion – Person who has an informal role and the vision to get the project started. The champion pushes for a project to be accepted where there are competing priorities and assists in keeping the project moving in spite of competition for resources.

Change Management - A process for managing scope through the use of formal change requests and reviews.

Charter – A formal document that describes the agreement between management, the Project Sponsor, and the PMO. It is the key document which describes the project and project scope. It includes descriptions of the processes, deliverables, resources, budget, roles and responsibilities, etc. Sometimes knows as work plan and Project initiation document.

Constraints - Specific management or technical limits that are part of the environment in which the project must be developed. Typical constraints include fixed deadlines, fixed resources, fixed costs, organizational standards, or fixed technology.

Critical Path - The group of tasks that aggregate to the longest time duration through the project constitute the critical path. These tasks have a set of inter-dependencies that result in a delay in one task on the critical path immediately delays all the other tasks on the critical path.

Critical Success Factors – "A limited number of concrete goals that must be met for the organization to be successful. Identifying these key factors helps determine the strategic directions and highlights the areas that can benefit from improved information systems[58]."

Culture - The totality of socially transmitted behavior patterns, arts, beliefs, institutions and all other products of human work and thought[59]

Deliverable - A tangible work product produced as output from tasks during a project, such as a project charter or a project work plan. Some tasks have deliverables such as reports or revised policy. Other tasks produce deliverables such as computer programs or new equipment.

Financial Management – Financial management consists of those policies and procedures necessary to maintain effective financial planning and reporting for the project.

Goal - A desire that states a direction toward which the project team will focus its efforts.

Integrated Test - A series of tests conducted to ensure that all of the systems, applications, interfaces, and procedures work together as designed.

Issue - A situation or unresolved matter that may impede the progress of a project.

Issue Management – This is a process for investigating, communicating, and resolving project issues.

Knowledge Transfer - Techniques for maintaining a program repository of key program work products and maintaining that consistency across projects. It is also a process for enabling the transfer of knowledge between team members during the course of a project.

Methodology - A pre-defined set of tasks that are designed to provide guidance or a check list for developing and implementing projects. The formal term "methodology" means the study of method.

Milestone – An identifiable step on the critical path of a project plan which is used as an interim measure of success.

Objective - Short-term target of defined and measurable achievement. It can also be described as a measurable step towards an established goal.

Package and Application Package - See Application Software

Phase - A unique set of activities producing one or more deliverables.

Program or Project Manager - Person with authority to manage a program. The Program Manager may also be responsible for one or more projects within a program. The Program Manager leads the overall planning and management of a program. All Project Managers within a program report to the Program Manager.

PMO - Project Management Office, Program Management Office - Sometimes used interchangeably, PMO includes responsibility for management of single, multiple, concurrent, related or unrelated projects. Each project may have its own Project Management as a subset of a Program Management Office.

Project – The term "project" referred to in this document, is assumed to mean the project for implementing a package software application, unless otherwise stated.

Project Life Cycle – The sum of phases and steps of a single project having a specific and identifiable beginning and end.

Project Management – The application of knowledge, skills, tools, and techniques to project activities in order to meet or exceed stakeholder needs and expectations from a project[60]. Managing the day-to-day and overall activities of an individual project. (Project Management and PMO are used interchangeably in this document, unless otherwise stated.)

Project Work Plan – A logically sequenced list of all steps, milestones, and phases required to complete a project. Detail line item data usually includes resources, dates, dependencies, duration, etc. Sometimes referred to as Project Plan or Work Breakdown Structure.

Quality - Fitness for the stated purpose.

Quality Assurance - The actions necessary to give confidence that a deliverable will satisfy the quality requirements.

Quality Management - A management approach with techniques for maintaining quality in the process and in deliverables from the process.

Quality Systems – Computer systems that do not break down, do the work intended, and are easy to maintain[61].

Regression Testing – Testing which includes a re-test of any bug fix as well as re-testing all previous fixes to ensure there is no impact on previously working code.

Release Management - A procedure for handling work requests, as well as scheduling and testing releases.

Resources – Situationally described as people or dollars expended toward project activities.

Resource Management - The direction and coordination of all resources throughout the project lifecycle, including budget and effective resource skill tracking and staffing.

Responsibility - The obligation to undertake a task.

Risk Assessment - Process to identify, characterize, and prioritize risks and mitigators for each risk that threatens the project team's ability to meet objectives within the agreed to scope, schedule, and budget.

Risk Management - A continuous process of identifying, analyzing, prioritizing, monitoring, and controlling project risks[62].

Scope – A quantitative definition of and limitations to the tasks to be performed during a project.

Scope Creep – A change in resources or requirements which may cause project scope, time, or budget to be exceeded.

Sponsor – Usually executive level individual or individuals who are responsible for providing resources to the project.

Stakeholder – "Anyone who has a vested interest in the project. This includes customers, financial managers, contributors, and so on[63]."

Step – An activity within a work plan. Usually the lowest level of line item detail used in a work plan.

System Test – A series of tests conducted upon the hardware and software (system), independent of related interfaces or applications. Usually undertaken prior to integration testing.

Work Plan – See Charter

Work Breakdown Structure – A deliverable-oriented grouping of project elements that organizes and defines the total work scope of the project. Each descending level represents an increasingly detailed definition of the project work. (*from PMBOC*)

REFERENCES

Bibliography

[1] *Bing, John, A, Principles of Project Management, P 40, PMNETwork, PMI, January 1994*

[2] *McNurlin, Barbara, C., Sprague, Jr. Ralph, H., Information Systems Management in Practice, P 278 - 279, Fourth Edition, Prentice-Hall, Inc., Saddle Brook, NJ, 1998*

[5] *Senge, Peter M...[et al.], The Fifth Discipline Fieldbook: Strategies and Tools for Building a Learning Organization, New York, Doubleday, 1995*

[4] *Saleem, Naveed, An Empirical Test Of The Contingency Approach To User Participation In Information Systems Development, P 145-166, Journal of Management Information Systems 13(1), 1996*

[5] *King, Julia, Project Management Ills Cost Businesses Plenty, Computerworld, Sept. 22, 1997*

[6] *Mingay, S., A Project Management Checklist, Gartner, HTTP://www.techweb.com, August 30, 2000*

[7] *Sullivan, George W., Planning for Successful Completion, Advance for Health Information Executives, July 2000*

[8] *Booth, Rose, IT Project Failures Costly, TechRepublic/Gartner Study, presented at Fifth Annual Project Leadership Conference, November 14, 2000*

[9] *Cafasso, Rosemary, Few IT Projects Come in on Time, on Budget, Computerworld, December 12, 1994*

[10] *Project Management Institute, Project Management Institute Body of Knowledge (PMBOK), 1999*

246 REFERENCES

[11] *Kyle, Mackenzie, Making IT Happen, A Non-Technical Guide to Project Management, P 40, John Wylie & Sons, Cnaada, Ltd., Ontario, Canada, 1998*

[12] *Greer, Michael, Handbook of Human Performance Technology, Chapter 6: Planning and Managing Human Performance Technology Projects, Jossey-Bass, San Francisco, 1999*

[13] *Light, Matt, A Strategic Analysis Report, P 3, Gartner Research, August, 2000*

[14] *Trepper, Charles, Getting an Edge on the Competition, P 69, Information Week, August 28, 2000*

[15] *Charvat, J., Project Management Methodologies, p3,4,John Wiley & Sons, NJ, 2003*

[16] *Projects in Controlled Environments (PRINCE), Project Management Methodology, Central Computer and Telecommunications Agency, United Kingdom, 1989*

[17] *Charvat, J., Project Management Methodologies, p33, John Wiley & Sons, NJ, 2003*

[18] *Davis, Michael, W., Developing Electronic Patient Information Systems, Computerizing Healthcare Information, P 77, McGraw-Hill, 1998*

[19] *Fitzgerald, Donna, Business Case Analysis: Tips and Techniques for Project Managers, Presentation at Project World 1998 - London, 1998*

[20] *Annex A. ISO/IEC 12207, (E) International Standard, Information Technology - Software Life Cycle Processes, 1995*

[21] Herzlich, Paul, Technical Director at Systeme Evolutif, quoted in "A Quality Argument", Computing, November 24, 1994

[22] Light, Matt, A Strategic Analysis Report, P 1, Gartner Research, August, 2000

[23] Ziv, Edward, A., Making Your Project a Success, P 52, Beyond Computing, October 2000

[24] Levine, Harvey, A., Does Your Company Need A CPO?, A Case for the Central Project Office and a Chief Project Officer, web site, http://www.pmforum.org/library/papers/Need_a_CPO.doc, 2001

[25] Melymuka, Kathleen, Born to Lead Projects, Computerworld, March 27, 2000

[26] Covey, Steven, Seven Habits of Highly Effective People, Covey Leadership Center, 1998

[27] Treasury Board of Canada Secretariat (TBS) IT Project Manager's Handbook Version 1.1, December, 1997

[28] Belzer, Kate, Businesses Need Programs to Implement Strategy, www.pmforum.org/library/papers/BusinessNeeds.htm, 2001

[29] Blanchard, Kenneth, Ph.D., Carew, Donald, Ed.D., Parisi-Carew, Eunice, Ed.D., The One Minute Manager, Builds High Performing Teams, P102, William Morrow and Company, Inc., New York, NY, 1990

[30] Ernst & Young LLP, PER Methodology, 1997

[31] Mahoney, J, Identify Misaligned Roles That Cause Project Failure, Gartner, September 13, 2000

[32] Thomsett, Rob, Into the Twilight Zone, P 8, 1998

[33] Wakin, Edward, Creating a Winning Team, P 62-63, Beyond Computing, October, 2000

[34] Kerzner, Harold, In Search of Excellence in Project Management, Successful Practices in High Performance Organizations, P 70, Van Nostrand Reinhold, United States, 1998

[35] Heller, Robert, Managing Teams, P 62, DK Publishing, Inc., 1998

[36] Post, Gerald, V., Anderson, David, I., Management Information Systems: Solving Business Problems With Information Technology, P 502, Second Edition, McGraw Hill, 2000

[37] Building Projects Practice Manual Core, Draft, P 2-13, June, 2000

[38] Stage PMC - Control Project Web Site, www.gantthead.com/Gantthead/process/processMain /1,1289,225-2110,00.html, April 2001

[39] Willcox, Graham, Morris, Steve, Successful Team Building, P 66, Hodder and Stroughton Educational, Great Britain, 1997

[40] Capezio, Peter, Winning Teams, Making Your Team Productive & Successful, P 66, National Press Publications, 1998

[41] Verzuh, Eric, The Fast Forward MBA in Project Management, P 57, John Wiley & Sons, New York, NY, 1999

[42] Anthes, Gary H., No More Creeps!, P 107, Computerworld, 1994

[43] *Reddy, Ram, Herding Cats Across the Supply Chain, P 47-48, Intelligent Enterprise, September 8, 2000*

[44] *Package-Enabled Reengineering, Implementation Phase, Implementation Wave/Site Preparation Stage, P 10-13, Ernst & Young Fusion Series, 1997*

[45] *Lewis, James, P., Mastering Project Management, Applying Advanced Concepts of Systems Thinking, Control and Evaluation, Resource Allocation, P 111, McGraw-Hill, New York, NY, 1998*

[46] *Mahoney, J., Identify Misaligned Roles That Cause Project Failure, Gartner, September 13, 2000*

[47] *Lewis, James, P., Mastering Project Management, Applying Advanced Concepts of Systems Thinking, Control and Evaluation, Resource Allocation, P 267-268, McGraw-Hill, New York, NY, 1998*

[48] *Capers Jones, Assessment and Control of Software Risks, Yourdon Press, 1994*

[49] *Sullivan, George, W., Planning for Successful Completion, P 24-25, Advance for Health Information Executives, July, 2000*

[50] *Kerzner, Harold, In Search of Excellence in Project Management, Successful Practices in High Performance Organizations, P 199-200, Van Nostrand Reinhold, United States, 1998*

[51] *Billows, Dick, Project and Program Management, Project Management Tiers, The Hampton Group, August, 1997*

[52] *Hampton Group, Managing Information Technology Projects, Chap 2, P 16, 2000*

[53] Crepeau, Neicole, Risk Assessment and Management, Microsoft Corporation, October, 1998

[54] Treasury Board of Canada Secretariat (TBS), IT Project Manager's Handbook Version 1.1, December, 1997

[55] Projects@work march/april 2002, 40 testing

[56] Mark Scheinberg, Ph.D., head of PlanView systems integration group, Writing software, PlanView, Inc, Austin, TX

[57] Davis, Michael, W., Developing Electronic Patient Information Systems, Computerizing Healthcare Information, P 85, McGraw-Hill, 1998

[58] Post, Gerald, V., Anderson, David, I., Management Information Systems: Solving Business Problems With Information Technology, P 642, Second Edition, McGraw Hill, 2000

[59] The American Heritage Dictionary of the English Language, Third Edition, Houghton Mifflin Company, Boston, Mass, 1992

[60] Mahoney, J., Identify Misaligned Roles That Cause Project Failure, Gartner, September 13, 2000

[61] McNurlin, Barbara, C., Sprague, Jr. Ralph, H., Information Systems Management in Practice, P 539, Fourth Edition, Prentice-Hall, Inc., Saddle Brook, NJ, 1998

[62] "Taxonomy-Based Risk Identification," Technical Report CMU/SEI-93-TR-6, June, 1993.

[63] Lewis, James, P., Mastering Project Management, Applying Advanced Concepts of Systems Thinking, Control and Evaluation, Resource Allocation, P 68, McGraw-Hill, New York, NY, 1998